SUMMER COOKING

FOR YEAR ROUND DINING

SUMMER COOKING
FOR YEAR ROUND DINING

CRESCENT BOOKS
New York

Published by Salamander Books Limited
129-137 York Way, London N7 9LG, United Kingdom

© Salamander Books Ltd., 1990

Reprinted 1991

Recipes and photographs on the following pages
are the copyright of Merehurst Press, and credited
as Bottom (B) or Top (T): 9 (B), 44, 123 (T), 132,
133, 134, 135, 136, 137, 138, 139, 140, 141, 142, 143

All correspondence concerning the content of this volume
should be addressed to Salamander Books Ltd.

This 1991 edition published by Crescent Books,
distributed by Outlet Book Company, Inc.,
a Random House Company,
225 Park Avenue South, New York, New York 10003.

Printed and bound in Italy

ISBN 0 517 06143 0

8 7 6 5 4 3 2 1

CREDITS

Designers: Sarah Cooper and Tim Scott

Contributing authors: Janice Murfitt, Cecilia Norman,
Lorna Rhodes, Louise Steele

Photographers: Paul Grater, Sue Jorgensen,
Jon Stewart

Typeset by: Maron Graphics Ltd., Wembley

Colour separation by: J. Film Process Ltd., Kentscan
Limited, Magnum Graphics Limited

CONTENTS

—INTRODUCTION—

Summer is the season of sunny days, warm evenings and tranquil nights. The chill winds of winter fade to become gentle breezes which stir the nodding blooms of wild flowers and garden beauties. The birds return from their southern wintering grounds to fill the woods and gardens with their cheerful songs. The world seems to become a more lively, more joyful place than it had been when storms ripped across the landscape.

It is the time of year when we take to the outdoors for our recreation and leisure. The gentle thud of tennis racket on ball is heard in many parks. Rivers come alive with pleasure boats and rowing boats.

With the warmer weather and brighter, outdoor style of living comes a new impetus in the kitchen. A whole range of exciting fruits and vegetables becomes available as the summer sun ripens the crops. The thick stews and satisfying puddings of winter begin to loose their appeal in the face of the new, lighter diet.

It is a time of great inspiration for the cook. A time to experiment, to innovate, to surprise. Equipped with the special summer ingredients and a little practical know-how it is possible to produce an endless succession of tantalizing, delicious dishes which will astound and amaze.

Warm, gentle evenings are ideal for barbecues. Few households cannot boast a barbecue and a collection of implements. With a little ingenuity a barbecue can be lifted out of the usual run of hamburgers and hot dogs to become a tempting and delicious feast. A few simple marinades can transform steaks and chops, while various sauces can be produced to suit any taste and dish. With very little effort the spontaneous barbecue can become a truly tempting feast.

Offering more scope to the imagination in food preparation is the traditional picnic. The archetypal *alfresco* meal may take place high on sunblown downs where the turf is springy and soft or in quiet meadows beside a lazily drifting river. A picnic may even be a great success in the back yard, especially with young children.

Wherever the picnic takes place it offers unrivaled opportunities for the production of tempting summer dishes. Sandwiches are the favorite and popular picnic fare with most people. They are also perhaps the easiest to make and offer greatest opportunities for experimentation. Fillings can be produced which include a vast range of ingredients. Savory anchovies, cheese and herbs can be blended together with mayonnaise or creams to form tasty moist fillings, while the simple slice of ham or beef can be livened up by a dash of mustard or relish.

Sandwiches need not take the form only of traditional filling between two slices of bread. There are open sandwiches and horn sandwiches to vary the shapes and so add increasing temptation to the spread. Indeed the various shapes can lead to fresh fillings. The horn sandwich is particularly suitable for stuffing with shrimps and other small items, while the sandwich roll lends itself to spreads and creamed mixes.

Salads, too, are favorite picnic dishes. The summer crops produce a whole host of ingredients which lend themselves particularly well to this use. The traditional salad vegetables of lettuce, tomato and cucumber can be used in conjunction with watercress, radishes and mushrooms to produce a tempting range of light snacks. It is even possible to add rose petals or dandelion leaves to green salads to give them an extra zing and excitement otherwise lacking. Dressings, too, can be the subject of experimentation and innovation. New combinations of standard pantry ingredients can produce surprisingly exotic and tempting dressings and the addition of a more unusual herb or flavoring can lift a simple green salad from the standard to the exceptional.

But picnic salads need not be simply variations on a theme. Pasta and potatoes lend themselves to use as more filling dishes. Requiring only a small amount of preparation, pasta and potato salads provide a base on which to build the lighter, more airy dishes of an outdoor meal. Even the hungriest child can be satisfied with a healthy portion of pasta salad. The inclusion of various other tempting ingredients and a range of herbs and spices can produce satisfying salads which will decorate the spread as well as nourish the eater.

Barbecues and picnics are the fun part of any summer diet, but cannot be indulged in every day of the week. Summer cooking is as much about daily meals as is winter cooking. And the range of ingredients available in the hot months is as suitable for sound healthy eating as it is for adventurous outdoor events. The salads and sandwiches which feature so highly on picnic menus can be favorites at family lunches and suppers. Indeed, they can be supplemented with a whole range of salads which are not difficult to transport, bringing fresh and exciting dishes to the table.

Nor need soups be ignored during the warm weather. Cold soups can be particularly refreshing, as well as nutritious. The familiar gazpacho is only one of tempting range of cold soups which can grace any table and need only the briefest of preparation.

But perhaps the most tempting items of all in summer cooking are the vast quantities of soft fruits which ripen to perfection on hot summer days. Strawberries, raspberries, and red currants all have their place in desserts for picnics, barbecues or more formal meals. Perhaps at their best when served fresh with a hint of sugar and lashings of cream, the soft fruits can also be used in a wide variety of dishes. Fruit salads and open tarts are tempting ways to serve such fruits, while light puddings and merigues can add variety. Sharper fruits, such as gooseberries, red currants and blackberries, are ideal for use in pies and pastries of various kinds. The blending of different fruits in cooked dishes is one of the finest arts of summer cooking, and can produce the most fascinating results.

The warm summer months offer unbounded opportunities to the adventurous cook. Opportunities for using seasonal ingredients, for new ways of presentation and for experiment which will give scope to the cook's creative talent. In this book are some of the most tempting dishes which can be produced during the hot days and evenings with a minimum of fuss and bother. There are dishes for every occasion, suggestions for experiment and exotic ingredients. Summer cuisine is perhaps the finest we have, and certainly the most enjoyable.

SOUPS

CHILLED FISH SOUP

SUMMER AVOCADO SOUP

1 pound shelled cooked shrimp
2 strips lemon peel
2 bay leaves
2 blades mace
salt and pepper
4 small squid, cleaned and gutted
2 scallions, green parts only, chopped
4 tomatoes, skinned, seeded and chopped
2 tablespoons peeled and chopped cucumber

Peel shrimp, putting shells, heads and tails into a saucepan. Reserve shrimp. Cover with 3¾ cups water and add lemon peel, bay leaves, mace and salt and pepper.

2 ripe avocados
3 teaspoons lemon juice
1 clove garlic, crushed
⅔ cup light cream
2½ cups cold chicken stock
dash hot-pepper sauce
salt and pepper
½ avocado, diced, and snipped fresh chives, to garnish

Halve avocados, discard seeds and scoop flesh into a blender or food processor. Add lemon juice, garlic and cream and work to a purée.

Bring to the boil, then cover and simmer for 30 minutes. Strain stock through a cheesecloth-lined strainer or coffee filter paper. Return stock to rinsed-out pan. Cut squid into thin rings and chop tentacles. Add to pan and cook for 5 minutes. Set aside to cool.

Blend in stock and season with hot-pepper sauce and salt and pepper.

Stir in scallions, tomatoes, cucumber and reserved shrimp. Season if necessary. Chill for at least 1 hour before serving.

Serves 4.

Turn into a bowl, cover with plastic wrap to prevent discoloration and chill for 1 hour. Serve garnished with diced avocado and snipped chives.

Serves 4-6.

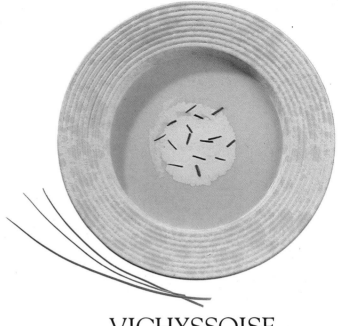

CLEAR BEET SOUP

VICHYSSOISE

1 onion, coarsely grated
1 large carrot, coarsely grated
1 pound raw beets, peeled and coarsely grated
parsley sprig
1 bay leaf
4 cups chicken stock
1 egg white
juice of ½ lemon
salt and pepper
thin strips lemon peel, to garnish

Put vegetables into a saucepan with herbs and stock. Bring to a boil, then cover and simmer for 30 minutes.

2 tablespoons butter
3 leeks, trimmed, sliced and washed
1 shallot, finely chopped
½ pound potatoes, sliced
3 cups light chicken stock
pinch ground mace or grated nutmeg
salt and pepper
⅔ cup light cream
snipped fresh chives, to garnish

Melt butter in a large saucepan, add leeks and shallot, then cover and cook gently for 10 minutes without browning. Add potatoes, chicken stock and mace or nutmeg.

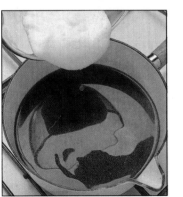

Strain soup and return it to rinsed-out pan. To clear soup, bring to a boil. Whisk egg white, then pour into pan and simmer gently for 15 minutes.

Bring to a boil, cover and simmer for 20 minutes. Purée in a blender or food processor, then pass through a strainer. Season with salt and pepper.

Strain soup through a cheesecloth-lined strainer into a bowl. Add lemon juice, then cool and chill. Season the soup before serving and garnish with thin strips of lemon peel.

Serves 4-6.

Set aside to cool, then stir in two-thirds of the cream. Chill until ready to serve. Ladle into bowls, swirl in remaining cream and garnish with snipped chives.

Serves 6.

CHILLED SCALLION SOUP

2 bunches scallions
1 tablespoon olive oil
3¾ cups vegetable stock
salt and pepper
1 hard-boiled egg, shelled, to garnish

Trim green tops from scallions and set aside. Chop white parts and add to a saucepan with oil, then sauté until soft.

Pour in stock and bring to a boil, then cover and simmer for 15 minutes.

Chop the green parts of scallions and add to soup. Cook for just 2 minutes, then set aside to cool. Chill and season with salt and pepper. Chop hard-boiled egg and sprinkle on to the soup to garnish.

Serves 4.

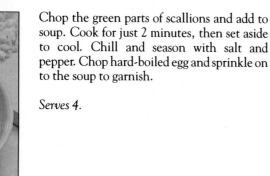

SOUP NORMANDE

2 tablespoons butter
1 Spanish onion, chopped
1 teaspoon mild curry powder
1 pound dessert apples
3 cups chicken stock
2 egg yolks
⅔ cup heavy cream
juice of ½ lemon
salt and pepper
mint leaves, to garnish

Melt butter in a large saucepan, add onion and cook gently until soft. Stir in curry powder.

Reserve 1 apple, then peel, core and chop remainder. Add to pan and cook for 1 minute. Pour in stock and bring to a boil, then cover and simmer for 20 minutes. Purée in a blender or food processor, then return to rinsed-out saucepan.

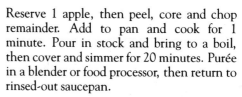

Beat egg yolks with cream and add to the soup, heating gently until thick. Do not boil. Cool, then chill for at least 2 hours. Peel, core and dice remaining apple and toss in lemon juice. Just before serving, add apple to soup, season and garnish each portion with mint leaves.

Serves 4-6.

COOL CHERRY SOUP

WATERCRESS & ALMOND SOUP

1 ½ pounds ripe black or red cherries
⅔ cup fruity white wine
cinnamon stick
2 tablespoons sugar
grated rind and juice of 1 lemon
1 ¼ cups thick sour cream
6 teaspoons brandy (optional)

2 large bunches watercress
2 tablespoons butter
1 small scallion, finely chopped
2 cups vegetable stock
⅓ cup blanched almonds, toasted and ground
4 teaspoons cornstarch
2 cups milk
salt and pepper
flaked almonds, lightly toasted, to garnish

Halve cherries with a knife and remove pit.
Put about half the pits into a strong plastic
bag and crush with a meat mallet.

Wash watercress and reserve a few sprigs for
garnish. Cut away any coarse stems and chop
remainder.

Put the crushed pits, whole pits and stems in a
saucepan. Add wine, cinnamon stick, sugar,
lemon rind and juice and ⅔ cup water. Bring
to a boil, cover and simmer for 10 minutes.
Strain and return to the pan with three-
quarters of the cherries and simmer for 5
minutes, until softened.

Melt butter in a saucepan, add scallion and
cook gently until soft. Add watercress and
cook for 2 minutes, then stir in stock, cover
and simmer for 10 minutes.

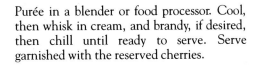

Purée in a blender or food processor. Cool,
then whisk in cream, and brandy, if desired,
then chill until ready to serve. Serve
garnished with the reserved cherries.

Serves 4-6.

Purée in a blender or food processor and
return to rinsed-out pan with the ground
almonds. Blend cornstarch with a little of the
milk, then add to pan with remaining milk
and cook gently over a low heat for 5
minutes, stirring, until smooth. Remove
from heat and set aside to cool. Refrigerate for
at least 4 hours or overnight. Season, then
serve garnished with a few toasted flaked
almonds sprinkled on top and the reserved
watercress sprigs.

Serves 4.

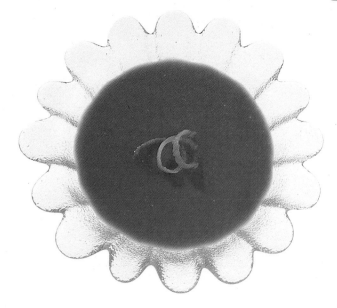

PEAR VICHYSSOISE

CHILLED PLUM SOUP

6 pears
juice of ½ lemon
3 cups chicken stock
1 leek, white part only, trimmed, chopped and washed
1 potato, chopped
½ teaspoon ground ginger
⅓ cup low-fat fromage frais
pinch grated nutmeg
salt and pepper
1 pear and watercress sprigs, to garnish

Peel and core the 6 pears, putting fruit into a bowl of water with lemon juice.

1 pound red plums, halved
⅔ cup fruity white wine
⅓ cup light brown sugar
1 tablespoon lemon juice
pinch ground cloves
⅔ cup buttermilk
½ teaspoon grated lemon peel
fine lemon rind twists, to garnish

Combine plums, wine, sugar, lemon juice, ground cloves and 2 cups water in a saucepan. Bring to a boil, then cover and simmer gently for about 10 minutes, until tender.

Put pear skins and cores into a saucepan with half the stock and simmer for a few minutes to extract all the flavor. Strain into a larger pan. Drain pears, chop coarsely and put into pan with leek, potato, remaining stock and ginger. Bring to a boil, then cover and simmer for 20 minutes, until vegetables are tender.

Strain through a strainer and discard skin and pits from plums.

Purée in a blender or food processor, then pour into a large bowl and set aside to cool, then chill. To serve, beat fromage frais into the soup, add nutmeg and salt and pepper and garnish with diced or sliced pear and sprigs of watercress.

Serves 4-6.

Set aside to cool, then stir in buttermilk and lemon peel. Chill the soup in freezer for 1 hour before serving. Serve icy cold, garnished with twists of lemon rind.

Serves 4-6.

CUCUMBER & YOGURT SOUP

LETTUCE SOUP

1 large cucumber
1 tablespoon olive oil
1 small onion, chopped
2½ cups hot chicken stock
grated peel and juice of ½ lemon
1 tablespoon chopped fresh dill
⅓ cup thick plain yogurt
salt and pepper
dill sprigs, to garnish

Cut 2-inch piece from cucumber, then chop remainder. Put oil in a pan, add onion and cook gently until soft.

2 plain round lettuces
1 tablespoon oil
1 bunch scallions, about 5 ounces, chopped
1 clove garlic, crushed
2 cups chicken stock
2 egg yolks
⅔ cup light cream
salt and pepper

Trim lettuces, discarding any damaged leaves, then separate and wash leaves. Reserve a few for garnish, then shred remaining leaves.

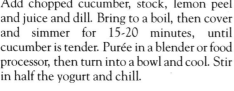

Add chopped cucumber, stock, lemon peel and juice and dill. Bring to a boil, then cover and simmer for 15-20 minutes, until cucumber is tender. Purée in a blender or food processor, then turn into a bowl and cool. Stir in half the yogurt and chill.

Heat oil in a large saucepan, add scallions and garlic and cook until tender. Add lettuce, cover and cook until wilted. Pour in stock and bring to a boil. Then re-cover and simmer for 15 minutes. Strain into a bowl.

Check seasoning, then thinly slice reserved piece of cucumber. Serve the soup garnished with thin slices of cucumber floating on the surface and the remaining yogurt spooned on top with sprigs of dill.

Serves 4-6.

Return soup to pan. Beat egg yolks and cream together and stir into soup, then cook over low heat until the soup thickens: do not boil. Cool soup, then chill. To serve, season, then roll up reserved lettuce leaves and slice finely to make a chiffonade. Stir into the soup as a garnish, then serve at once.

Serves 4.

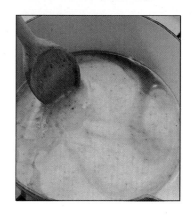

FINNISH BERRY SOUP

ICED FENNEL SOUP

1½ pounds fresh or frozen mixed berries, such as
   raspberries, red currants, black currants
1 cup sweet white wine
cinnamon stick
¼ cup sugar
½ cup whipping cream, to garnish

Select a few of the best raspberries for
garnishing and reserve. Put remaining fruit in
a pan with the wine, cinnamon stick, sugar
and 2 cups water. Simmer for 5-10 minutes,
stirring occasionally, until fruit is soft.

2 fennel bulbs, about 1 pound
1 tablespoon sunflower oil
1 small onion, chopped
3 cups chicken or vegetable stock
⅔ cup thick sour cream
salt and pepper

Remove the green feathery fronds from
fennel and reserve. Roughly chop bulbs. Put
oil into a saucepan over a medium heat, add
fennel and onion, then cover and cook gently
for 10 minutes.

Discard cinnamon stick and strain the soup
through a fine strainer.

Add stock and bring to a boil, then reduce
heat and simmer for about 20 minutes or until
the fennel is tender.

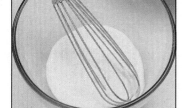

Cool, then chill for at least 1 hour before
serving. To serve, lightly whip the cream and
swirl on to the soup, then top with the
reserved raspberries.

Serves 6.

Purée the soup in a blender or food processor.
Cool, then beat in sour cream and season
with salt and pepper. Chill and check
seasoning again before serving, garnished
with reserved fennel fronds.

Serves 6.

ICED MELON SOUP

SUMMER TOMATO BISQUE

2 different colored melons, weighing about 1½ pounds each, such as galia, cantaloupe, honeydew
knob fresh ginger root, peeled
½ cup sugar
1 cup dry white wine

Cut each melon in half and discard seeds. Scoop out a few small balls from the green (galia) melon and set aside. Scoop out the remaining flesh from melons, keeping both varieties separate.

2 pounds ripe tomatoes, chopped
3 scallions, chopped
½ red pepper, seeded and chopped
2 cloves garlic, crushed
2 cups vegetable stock
1 teaspoon sugar
2 tablespoons chopped fresh basil
¼ cup crème fraîche or plain yogurt
salt and pepper
1 avocado and snipped fresh chives, to garnish

Put tomatoes, scallions, red pepper and garlic in a saucepan with stock and sugar.

Put 2½ cups water in a saucepan with ginger and sugar and simmer for 5 minutes. Cool, then remove ginger. Put half of the wine into a blender or food processor with one variety of melon flesh and pour in half the cooled syrup. Blend, then pour into a bowl. Repeat with remaining wine and syrup and other melon flesh.

Bring to a boil, then cover and simmer for 15 minutes. Remove from heat and leave to cool. Purée in a blender or food processor, then strain into a bowl. Cover and chill for 2 hours. Stir in the basil, crème fraîche or yogurt and add salt and pepper.

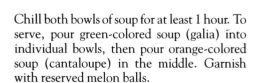

Chill both bowls of soup for at least 1 hour. To serve, pour green-colored soup (galia) into individual bowls, then pour orange-colored soup (cantaloupe) in the middle. Garnish with reserved melon balls.

Serves 4-6.

Halve avocado and discard seed, peel and slice. Ladle soup into individual bowls, arrange avocado slices on top, then sprinkle with snipped chives and serve.

Serves 6.

GAZPACHO

SENEGALESE SOUP

1 pound ripe tomatoes, skinned and chopped
½ cucumber, peeled and chopped
1 green pepper, seeded and chopped
1 red pepper, seeded and chopped
1 small onion, chopped
1 clove garlic, chopped
1 cup soft bread crumbs
2 tablespoons olive oil
2 tablespoons red wine vinegar
2 cups tomato juice
½ teaspoon dried marjoram
salt and pepper

Put all soup ingredients into a blender or food processor, in 2 batches if necessary.

2 tablespoons butter
1 small onion, chopped
2 teaspoons mild curry powder
2 tablespoons all-purpose flour
4 cups chicken stock
juice of ½ lemon
⅔ cup light cream or plain yogurt
4 ounces cooked skinless chicken breast fillet, cut into thin strips
cilantro leaves, to garnish

Melt butter in a saucepan, then add onion and cook gently until soft.

Blend until smooth. The soup should be the consistency of light cream; if it is too thick add a little iced water. Turn the soup into a bowl, cover and refrigerate for about 2 hours before serving.

Stir in curry powder and flour and cook for 1 minute. Stir in chicken stock and bring to a boil, then simmer for 4 minutes. Strain soup through a strainer into a bowl. Set aside to cool.

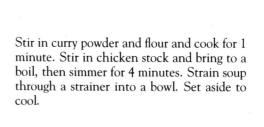

When the soup is well chilled, season if necessary and add few ice cubes.

Serves 4-6.

Note: Gazpacho is traditionally served with a selection of garnishes handed around separately to be added to individual portions as desired. Put 2 chopped hard-boiled eggs, finely diced ½ cucumber, finely chopped onion, 12 pitted and chopped green or ripe olives and 1 diced green pepper into separate small bowls.

Whisk in lemon juice and cream or yogurt. Stir in chicken and chill for a few hours. Serve well chilled, garnished with cilantro leaves.

Serves 4-6.

Variation: Add 4 ounces shelled cooked shrimp, coarsely chopped, instead of the strips of chicken.

DRESSINGS

VINAIGRETTE DRESSING

½ teaspoon salt
pepper
½ teaspoon Dijon mustard
½ teaspoon sugar
2 tablespoons wine vinegar
⅓ cup olive oil

Put salt, pepper, mustard, sugar and vinegar into a bowl and stir together until salt and sugar have dissolved.

Pour in oil and beat with a fork to combine well.

Alternatively, place ingredients in a screw-top jar and shake well until blended.

Makes about ½ cup.

Note: Use less oil if a sharper dressing is preferred. Use cider or herb-flavored vinegar, or substitute lemon juice for the wine vinegar.

VARIATIONS

For Garlic Vinaigrette: Add 1 or 2 crushed cloves of garlic to the dressing.

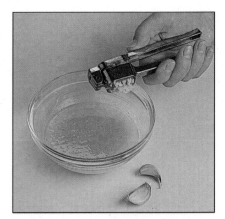

For Herb Vinaigrette: Add 1-2 tablespoons of chopped fresh herbs, such as parsley, chervil, basil, tarragon or chives, or a mixture.

For Honey Vinaigrette: Substitute 1 teaspoon clear honey for the sugar in the dressing.

For Light Vinaigrette: Replace half or all of the olive oil with sunflower oil.

MAYONNAISE

1 egg yolk
pinch salt
½ teaspoon Dijon mustard
⅔ cup olive oil
2 tablespoons wine vinegar or lemon juice

Have all the ingredients at room temperature: this will help prevent curdling. Put egg yolk, salt and mustard into a bowl. Stand bowl on a damp cloth to stop it sliding about.

Whisk ingredients together, then begin to add oil, drop by drop, whisking all the time.

As mayonnaise thickens, add oil in a steady trickle. When all oil has been added, beat in vinegar or lemon juice. The mayonnaise can be thinned by the addition of a little hot water, if necessary.

Makes ⅔ cup.

VARIATIONS

For Quicker Blender Mayonnaise: Using the same ingredients, put the egg yolk, salt and mustard into a blender. Work for 15 seconds, then add oil slowly, quickening as the mayonnaise thickens. Work in the vinegar, then season, if necessary.

For Herb Mayonnaise: Add 2 tablespoons chopped fresh herbs, such as parsley, chives or tarragon, or a mixture.

For Garlic Mayonnaise (Aïoli): Add 2 crushed cloves of garlic to the egg yolk before adding the oil.

For Light Mayonnaise: Replace either half or all the olive oil with sunflower oil, and whisk in 2 tablespoons plain yogurt.

ALMOND YOGURT DRESSING

⅓ cup blanched almonds, ground
2 cloves garlic, crushed
¼ teaspoon salt
½ teaspoon black pepper
1 teaspoon grated lime peel
¼ cup almond oil
2 tablespoons white wine
½ cup low-fat plain yogurt
2 teaspoons chopped fresh lovage
2 teaspoons chopped fresh oregano
2 teaspoons chopped fresh parsley

Put ground almonds, garlic, salt, pepper, lime peel and almond oil in a bowl and stir together with a wooden spoon until well mixed.

Stir in wine and yogurt and beat together until blended. Cover with plastic wrap and leave in a cool place until required.

Add chopped herbs and stir well. Serve with a grated carrot and celeriac salad, mixed cooked green or lima beans or mixed rice and pasta salads which include meat and fish.

Makes ⅔ cup.

Variations: Replace the almonds with Brazil, pine or pistachio nuts, finely ground.

EGG & WALNUT DRESSING

2 hard-boiled eggs, peeled and roughly chopped
1 teaspoon light soft brown sugar
¼ teaspoon cayenne pepper
1 teaspoon Dijon mustard
1 teaspoon dry mustard
¼ cup walnut oil
1 tablespoon cider vinegar
½ cup thick yogurt
1 tablespoon chopped walnuts

Press eggs through a strainer over a bowl using a wooden spoon, or blend in a food processor.

Add sugar, cayenne pepper, mustards and oil and beat until well blended. Stir in vinegar and beat until cloudy and slightly thick. Stir in yogurt and walnuts until well mixed. Cover the dressing with plastic wrap and leave in a cool place until required.

Serve this piquant dressing with all meat and fish dishes, hot or cold. Mix together with cold rice and pasta as a base for a meat, fish or vegetable salad.

Makes ⅔ cup.

Variation: Add 4 teaspoons chopped fresh mixed herbs and replace walnut oil and walnuts with hazelnut oil and hazelnuts.

ORANGE & HERB YOGURT

HERBED VERMOUTH DRESSING

1 teaspoon finely grated orange peel
2 tablespoons freshly squeezed orange juice
1 clove garlic, crushed
1/4 cup sunflower oil
1/2 cup thick yogurt
2 teaspoons chopped fresh rosemary
2 teaspoons chopped fresh cilantro
2 teaspoons chopped fresh parsley

Put orange peel and juice, garlic and oil in a bowl and beat with wooden spoon until well blended. Stir in yogurt.

Cover with plastic wrap and leave in a cool place until required. Stir in the chopped mixed herbs and serve at once.

Use this light dressing with sliced beets, chopped cucumber, potato and cooked vegetable salads and any curried dish.

Makes 2/3 cup.

Variations: Replace orange peel and juice with lime, lemon or grapefruit peel and juice, or raspberry, strawberry or currant juices.

1/4 teaspoon dry mustard
1/4 teaspoon salt
1/2 teaspoon black pepper
1/2 teaspoon light soft brown sugar
1/2 cup grapeseed oil
2 tablespoons sweet red or dry white vermouth
2 teaspoons chopped fresh purple basil
1 teaspoon chopped fresh hyssop
1 teaspoon chopped fresh dill

Place mustard, salt, pepper, sugar and oil in a bowl and beat together until well blended.

Add vermouth and beat until cloudy and slightly thick. Cover with plastic wrap and leave in a cool place until required.

Just before using, stir in basil, hyssop and dill. Serve with a mushroom, apple, nut and celery salad, or marinate mushrooms and thin slices or chunks of melon in this dressing for 1-2 hours in a cool place, then serve as an appetizer.

Makes 2/3 cup.

Variations: Replace vermouth with elderflower wine and herbs with 4 teaspoons elderflower heads. Add 3 teaspoons chopped fresh mint instead of the herbs.

TOMATO & OLIVE DRESSING

2 tomatoes, weighing about 4 ounces	
¼ teaspoon salt	
½ teaspoon black pepper	
1 teaspoon sugar	
½ cup thick yogurt	
8 ripe olives, chopped	
1 tablespoon chopped fresh parsley	
1 tablespoon chopped fresh chervil	

Plunge tomatoes into boiling water for 30 seconds, then pierce skins and peel off. Halve tomatoes and remove seeds.

Press tomatoes through a strainer or place in a food processor fitted with a metal blade. Process tomatoes until puréed.

Stir in salt, pepper, sugar and yogurt until well blended. Cover with plastic wrap and leave in a cool place until required. Add olives and herbs and stir to blend well.

Serve with a celery, apple and potato salad, or a salad of cauliflower and broccoli flowerets mixed with chopped walnuts.

Makes ⅔ cup.

MINT & RASPBERRY DRESSING

2 tablespoons chopped fresh mint	
1 tablespoon light soft brown sugar	
½ cup grapeseed oil	
⅓ cup raspberries	
2 tablespoons raspberry vinegar	
2 teaspoons pink peppercorns, crushed	

Put mint, sugar and 1 tablespoon boiling water in a bowl and stir until sugar has dissolved. Leave to cool.

Using a wooden spoon, stir in oil until well blended. Place a strainer over the bowl and, using a wooden spoon, press raspberries through so only the seeds remain in strainer.

Add vinegar and peppercorns and beat until evenly blended. Cover with plastic wrap and leave in a cool place until required.

Serve with any mixed salad ingredients, including artichokes, avocado, lamb, chicken, duck, salmon or trout.

Makes ⅔ cup.

Variations: Replace raspberries with the same quantity of loganberries, blackberries, strawberries, red currants or black currants.

SUNSET DRESSING

¼ teaspoon salt
½ teaspoon ground black pepper
1 teaspoon Dijon mustard
½ cup grapeseed oil
4 teaspoons Grenadine syrup
2 tablespoons black currant wine vinegar
2 tablespoons chopped fresh basil

Put salt, pepper, mustard and oil in a bowl and beat together until well mixed.

Add Grenadine syrup and black currant vinegar and beat until mixture has blended well together.

Stir in the basil and pour dressing into a glass serving pitcher or dish. Cover with plastic wrap and leave in a cool place. The dressing will separate into several layers from pale yellow to deep red with herbs suspended in the middle. Stir just before pouring.

Use to pour over mixed salads of all kinds. It is especially good with avocado and orange salad, cold meat and mixed salads or celery root, carrot and Jerusalem artichokes.

Makes ⅔ cup.

Variation: Replace black currant vinegar and chopped fresh basil with raspberry vinegar and a few fresh or frozen raspberries.

SWEET & SOUR DRESSING

1 shallot, finely chopped
1 clove garlic, crushed
¼ teaspoon salt
½ teaspoon black pepper
½ teaspoon paprika
2 teaspoons French mustard
4 teaspoons light soft brown sugar
1 teaspoon Worcestershire sauce
1 tablespoon tomato paste
½ cup olive oil
⅓ cup black currant vinegar
¼ yellow pepper
¼ red pepper

Put shallot, garlic, salt, pepper, paprika, mustard, sugar, Worcestershire sauce, tomato paste and oil in a bowl. Beat with a wooden spoon until well blended.

Add vinegar and beat until cloudy and slightly thick. Cover with plastic wrap and leave in a cool place until ready to use.

Place peppers under a hot broiler, skin side uppermost, until skin has charred and bubbled. Peel off skins and chop peppers finely, then set aside until cold.

Add peppers to dressing and stir until well blended.

Serve with mixed rice salad or a cabbage, apple and onion salad.

Makes ⅔ cup.

GRAPEFRUIT GINGER DRESSING

2 teaspoons finely grated grapefruit rind
¼ teaspoon salt
¼ teaspoon black pepper
¼ teaspoon dry mustard
½ cup almond oil
2 tablespoons ginger wine
2 tablespoons freshly squeezed grapefruit juice

Put grapefruit rind, salt, pepper, mustard and oil in a bowl and mix together with a wooden spoon until well blended.

Add ginger wine and grapefruit juice and beat until cloudy and slightly thick. Cover with plastic wrap and leave in a cool place until ready to use. Beat before serving.

Serve with a red cabbage and apple salad, or beets and celery.

Makes ⅔ cup.

Variations: Substitute orange, lemon or lime peel and juice for the grapefruit. Add 4-5 teaspoons chopped fresh mint or rosemary to give added flavor and color.

WALNUT DRESSING

1 teaspoon light soft brown sugar
1 teaspoon Dijon mustard
¼ teaspoon salt
½ teaspoon black pepper
½ cup walnut oil
2 tablespoons cider vinegar
1 tablespoon finely chopped walnuts
1 tablespoon chopped fresh sage

Put sugar, mustard, salt, pepper and walnut oil in a bowl. Beat together until well blended.

Add cider vinegar and beat until cloudy and slightly thick. Cover with plastic wrap and leave in a cool place until required.

Stir in walnuts and sage and serve with a mixed hot or cold pasta salad of peppers, onions, corn and pasta.

Makes ⅔ cup.

Variations: Replace the walnut oil and walnuts with peanut oil and finely chopped peanuts, almond oil and almonds or hazelnut oil and hazelnuts.

CELERY ROOT & FENNEL DRESSING

CREAMY EGGPLANT DRESSING

⅓ cup grated celery root
1 tablespoon chopped scallion
2 tablespoons chopped fennel bulb
1 tablespoon chopped fennel leaves
¼ teaspoon salt
½ teaspoon black pepper
¼ teaspoon dry mustard
1 teaspoon clear honey
2 tablespoons green peppercorn vinegar
⅔ cup thick soured cream

Put celery root, scallions, fennel bulb and leaves, salt, pepper, mustard and honey in a bowl and mix well together using a wooden spoon. Stir in vinegar and soured cream, then stir until well blended.

Cover with plastic wrap and leave in a cool place until required.

Serve with cold meats and fish or with a potato and bacon salad, a mixed three-bean salad or cold pasta.

Makes about 1¼ cups.

Variations: Replace celery root with 2 tablespoons grated fresh horseradish or extra strong horseradish sauce.

1 small eggplant, about 10 ounces
1 clove garlic, crushed
¼ teaspoon cayenne pepper
¼ teaspoon salt
¼ teaspoon dry mustard
⅔ cup thick soured cream
4 teaspoons chopped fresh cilantro or tarragon

Place eggplant under a hot broiler or in a preheated oven at 400F. Cook, turning occasionally, for 15-20 minutes, until skin has charred and flesh is soft. Cool slightly, then peel off skin and place flesh in a food processor fitted with a metal blade; process until puréed. Alternatively, press eggplant through a strainer using a wooden spoon.

Blend in garlic, cayenne pepper, salt, mustard and soured cream until dressing is smooth.

Cover with plastic wrap and leave in a cool place until required. Just before serving, stir in cilantro or tarragon.

Use as a mayonnaise to accompany all types of salads.

Makes about 1¼ cups.

Note: This dressing can also be used as a dip with fresh sticks of vegetables. Creamy in texture, it is also good for coating new potatoes, cooked mixed vegetables, hard-boiled eggs and tuna chunks.

DILL & CUCUMBER DRESSING

2-inch piece cucumber
¼ teaspoon salt
1 tablespoon chopped fresh dill
2 teaspoons snipped fresh chives
¼ teaspoon paprika
1 teaspoon finely grated orange peel
1 tablespoon orange juice
⅔ cup thick soured cream

Peel cucumber, cut into ¼-inch dice, then place in a bowl and sprinkle with salt. Leave for 30 minutes in a cool place.

Meanwhile, in a bowl, mix dill, chives, paprika, orange peel and juice and soured cream together.

Stir until evenly blended. Cover with plastic wrap and leave in a cool place until required.

Drain cucumber, pat dry on paper towels, then stir into soured cream mixture.

Serve with potato salad or with cold mixed cooked vegetables such as cauliflower, beans, peas and zucchini.

Makes about ⅔ cup.

Variation: Replace the dill with other fresh herbs, such as chopped mint, thyme or basil.

LENTIL DRESSING

⅓ cup red lentils
¼ teaspoon salt
½ teaspoon black pepper
¼ teaspoon grated nutmeg
1 tablespoon snipped fresh chives
⅔ cup thick soured cream

Put lentils in a saucepan with 1¼ cups boiling water, cover and simmer for 20 minutes, until all water has been absorbed.

Pass lentils through a fine strainer using a wooden spoon, or place in food processor fitted with a metal blade and process until puréed.

Stir in salt, pepper, nutmeg, chives and soured cream until evenly mixed, or blend in a food processor for a few seconds.

Cover with plastic wrap and leave in cool place until required. Serve with hard-boiled eggs, anchovies and olives, or with cold meats and cold cooked fish.

Makes about ⅔ cup.

Variation: For a thinner dressing, add freshly squeezed orange juice, or for a sharper flavor use vinegar.

APPLE & MADEIRA DRESSING

1 cooking apple, about 10 ounces,
peeled, cored and grated

1 teaspoon light soft brown sugar

⅓ cup sunflower oil

¼ cup Madeira

Put apple in a saucepan with ⅓ cup water and bring to a boil; cook gently until tender.

Press apple through a strainer over a bowl using a wooden spoon, or process in a food processor fitted with a metal blade until puréed. Stir in sugar and leave mixture until cold.

Beat in oil and Madeira until well blended. Cover with plastic wrap and chill until required.

Serve with a cold pork and rice salad, mixed pasta or hot pork, poultry or game birds.

Makes 1 cup.

Variation: Add 3-4 teaspoons chopped fresh apple mint to the dressing just before serving.

CHERRY CINNAMON DRESSING

1 cup sweet cherries, pitted

⅓ cup rosé wine

¼ teaspoon ground cinnamon

1 teaspoon sugar

⅓ cup grapeseed oil

Put cherries, wine and cinnamon in a saucepan. Bring to a boil, cover and cook very gently for 2-3 minutes, until cherries are tender.

Press cherries through a strainer into a bowl using a wooden spoon, or using a food processor fitted with a metal blade process cherries until puréed. Leave until cold.

Beat in or process sugar and oil until thick and smooth. Cover with plastic wrap and chill the dressing until required.

Serve with a cold duck, goose or pheasant salad or hot poultry or game. Mix together with apple, celery, nuts and peppers for a salad.

Makes about ⅔ cup.

EGG & MUSTARD DRESSING

2 hard-boiled egg yolks, pushed through a strainer
1 egg yolk
2 teaspoons dry mustard
2 tablespoons olive oil
1 teaspoon Worcestershire sauce
1 teaspoon white wine vinegar
2 scallions, finely chopped
⅔ cup whipping cream

Put hard-boiled and raw egg yolks and mustard in a bowl and beat together with a wooden spoon.

Beat in oil drop by drop until all oil is incorporated and mixture is smooth. Stir in Worcestershire sauce, vinegar and scallions.

Whip cream until thick, then add to egg mixture and fold in gently until mixture is well blended. Cover with plastic wrap and chill until ready to serve.

Serve as an accompaniment to cold beef, pork or chicken salads or use as a substitute for mayonnaise when making egg salad.

Makes 1 cup.

Variations: For Lemon Mustard Dressing: Replace vinegar with lemon juice and add 1 teaspoon finely grated lemon peel, 1 teaspoon clear honey and 1 tablespoon chopped fresh herbs. Mix in well before adding cream.

SMOKED SEAFOOD DRESSING

2 smoked trout fillets, about 4 ounces, skinned
2 teaspoons finely grated lime peel
2 tablespoons freshly squeezed lime juice
⅔ cup light cream
1 tablespoon snipped fresh chives
2 tablespoons chopped fresh watercress
¼ teaspoon cayenne pepper
lime wedges, to garnish

Place trout in a food processor fitted with a metal blade, add lime peel and juice and process until smooth.

Add light cream and process again until well blended. Stir in chives, watercress and cayenne. Place in a serving dish and garnish with lime wedges.

Serve with any seafood salad or with broiled fish. This also makes a good accompaniment to a mixed vegetable or leaf salad

Makes 1 cup.

Variation: Replace smoked trout fillets with either smoked salmon or mackerel fillets.

APPETIZERS

CEVICHE

1 pound fish fillets, such as flounder, cod, lemon sole, mackerel or bass

juice of 5 limes

2 tablespoons olive oil

2 cloves garlic, finely chopped

3 tomatoes, skinned, seeded and chopped

1 green chili, seeded and finely chopped

1 onion, finely chopped

12 green olives, pitted

2 tablespoons chopped fresh cilantro

salt and pepper

½ avocado

lime slices and cilantro leaves, to garnish

Skin fish, cut into thin slices or small chunks. Place in a glass dish and pour over lime juice. Cover and refrigerate for 24 hours.

Next day, heat oil, cook garlic until colored slightly. Remove from heat, leave to cool, then add tomatoes, chili, onion, olives and cilantro. Season with salt and pepper.

Drain fish, add to sauce, making sure all the fish is well coated, then cover bowl and chill.

To serve, divide fish and sauce between 4 dishes. Peel and slice avocado. Place a few slices on each plate.

Garnish with lime slices and cilantro leaves.

Serves 4.

SEAFOOD IN WINE GELATIN

1 salmon steak, 6 ounces, cut in half

12 queen scallops or 6 medium scallops

1½ cups dry white wine

salt and white pepper

1 cup fish stock, strained

1 tablespoon unflavored gelatin

6 ounces shelled cooked shrimp

dill sprigs

SAFFRON DRESSING:

1 tablespoon olive oil

1 shallot, chopped

pinch saffron threads

3 tablespoons heavy cream

Put salmon and scallops into a pan with ⅔ cup of the wine. Season with salt and pepper, then simmer for 5-6 minutes. Allow fish to cool in cooking liquid.

Pour half the stock into bowl. Sprinkle gelatin over and leave to soften for 2-3 minutes. Stand bowl in a saucepan of hot water; stir until dissolved. Add remaining stock and wine; spoon 1 tablespoon into six ½-cup capacity oval molds. Refrigerate until set.

Lift cooled fish out of pan, reserving cooking liquid. Cut salmon into small pieces; slice scallops. Layer up the fish, shrimp and dill in each mold. Pour over a little gelatin mixture as layers build up. Refrigerate until set.

To make dressing, heat oil in a small pan, cook shallot for 2 minutes, add cooking liquid from fish and simmer for 5 minutes. Place saffron threads in a bowl, then pour the hot fish liquid over and leave to cool.

Turn out on to a serving plate. Strain saffron mixture and beat in cream. Pour a little around each mold and serve garnished with any remaining shrimp and dill.

Serves 6.

CAESAR SALAD

⅓ cup olive oil	
2 cloves garlic, halved	
4 thick slices bread	
1 Cos lettuce	
6 anchovy fillets, chopped	
¼ cup grated Parmesan cheese	
SOFT EGG DRESSING:	
1 egg	
5 teaspoons lemon juice	
3 tablespoons olive oil	
1 teaspoon Worcestershire sauce	
¼ teaspoon Dijon mustard	
salt and pepper	

Place oil in a bowl with garlic; leave for 1 hour, then remove garlic.

Toast bread, remove crusts and cut into squares. Heat garlic-flavored oil in a skillet. Add bread cubes and fry until crisp and golden, turning frequently. Lift out croutons and drain on paper towels.

To assemble salad, tear most of the lettuce into large pieces, reserving a few small inner leaves whole. Arrange whole leaves around edge of a salad bowl. Put torn lettuce in the center with croutons, anchovies and Parmesan cheese.

To make dressing, boil egg for 1 minute. Crack open into a bowl, scraping out from the shell. Add remaining ingredients, seasoning to taste with salt and pepper, and until smooth.

Pour dressing over salad and toss gently. Serve immediately.

Serves 4.

SMOKED SALMON NESTS

2 sheets phyllo pastry	
2 tablespoons butter, melted	
2 ounces chicory	
1-inch piece cucumber	
4 ounces smoked salmon	
2 tablespoons Lemon Vinaigrette	

Pre-heat oven to 400F. Cut phyllo pastry into twelve 3½-inch squares. Brush with butter and place in 4 individual muffin pans, putting 3 pieces in each. Gently press into pans, then bake for 10 minutes until crisp and golden. Leave to cool.

Put chicory into a bowl. Cut cucumber into short batons and salmon into strips. Add to bowl with dressing and toss well. Pile into pastry cases and serve at once.

Serves 4.

LEEKS À LA GREQUE

1 pound young leeks
¼ cup olive oil
1 onion, finely chopped
3 tomatoes, skinned, seeded and chopped
1 clove garlic, crushed
⅔ cup dry white wine
12 coriander seeds, slightly crushed
1 bay leaf
pinch cayenne pepper
salt and pepper
2 teaspoons chopped fresh thyme
chopped ripe olives and thyme, to garnish

Wash and trim leeks. Cut into 2-inch pieces, then blanch in a saucepan of boiling water for 2 minutes. Drain and set aside.

Heat 3 tablespoons oil in a large saucepan. Add onion and 1 table-spoon water and cook gently for 8 minutes. Add tomatoes, garlic, wine, coriander seeds, bay leaf and cayenne pepper. Season with salt and pepper and cook for about 15 minutes, or until tomatoes are pulpy. Add leeks and cook, un-covered, for 10-15 minutes until tender. If sauce is getting dry, add a little water.

Discard bay leaf, then allow mixture to cool. Transfer to a serving dish, sprinkle over thyme and chill until needed.

To serve, drizzle remaining oil over leeks and garnish with chopped olives and thyme.

Serves 4.

MARINATED MUSHROOMS

2 tablespoons olive oil
1 shallot, finely chopped
4 ounces shiitake mushrooms, stems removed and sliced if large
⅓ cup dry white wine
4 ounces button mushrooms, trimmed
4 ounces oyster mushrooms
1 teaspoon pink peppercorns in brine, drained
1 teaspoon green peppercorns in brine, drained
3 tablespoons walnut oil
½ teaspoon Dijon mustard
salt
1 teaspoon chopped fresh oregano
watercress sprigs, to garnish

Heat olive oil in a skillet and cook shallot for 2 minutes. Add shiitake mushrooms, sauté for 2-3 minutes, then pour wine over and simmer for 2 minutes. Remove from heat, turn into a bowl and leave to cool.

Slice button mushrooms and halve oyster mushrooms if large. Strain the marinating liquid from shiitake mushrooms into a small bowl. Mix all the mushrooms together in a bowl with pepper-corns.

Beat walnut oil and mustard into cooking liquid and season with salt. Pour over mushrooms and stir together. Sprinkle oregano over the top and leave to marinate for up to 1 hour before serving garnished with watercress.

Serves 4.

SMOKED FISH PLATTER

2 smoked trout fillets

2 peppered smoked mackerel fillets

3 slices bread, toasted

2 tablespoons butter

1 teaspoon lemon juice

3½-ounce can smoked oysters, drained

small lettuce leaves, lemon slices and

parsley or dill, to garnish

HORSERADISH SAUCE:

3 tablespoons thick strained yogurt

2 teaspoons horseradish relish

1 teaspoon lemon juice

2 teaspoons chopped fresh parsley

pepper

Skin trout and mackerel fillets and carefully cut them into small even-sized pieces. Set them aside.

Using a small fancy cutter, cut out 4 circles from each toast. Beat butter and lemon juice together. Spread a little on the toast circles. Place a smoked oyster on each buttered toast circle.

Arrange the pieces of smoked fish and the oysters on toast on 4 plates. Garnish each plate with a few lettuce leaves, lemon slices and parsley or dill.

Make sauce by mixing ingredients together in a bowl. Spoon into a serving dish and serve with salads.

Serves 4.

JELLIED GAZPACHO SALAD

1 pound tomatoes, skinned, seeded and chopped

1 small onion, chopped

1 clove garlic, crushed

½ teaspoon celery salt

1 teaspoon tomato paste

1 teaspoon white wine vinegar

1 tablespoon unflavored gelatin

salt and pepper

TO FINISH:

3-inch piece cucumber, peeled and diced

¼ Spanish onion, finely diced

½ green pepper, seeded and diced

2 sticks celery, diced

cress, to garnish

Put tomatoes, onion, garlic, celery salt, tomato paste and vinegar into a saucepan and simmer until soft and pulpy. Strain mixture into a measuring jug.

Sprinkle gelatin over ¼ cup water in a small bowl and leave to soften for 2-3 minutes. Stand bowl in a saucepan of hot water and stir until dissolved. Allow to cool, then stir into the tomato mixture, making up to 2½ cups with water if necessary. Season with salt and pepper. Pour into 4 individual ⅔-cup ring molds and refrigerate until set.

To turn out, dip each mold into a bowl of hot water for a few seconds, then invert on to a serving plate.

Arrange diced vegetables around each and serve garnished with cress.

Serves 4.

ITALIAN SEAFOOD SALAD

2 pounds fresh mussels, scrubbed and bearded

1 pound fresh clams, scrubbed

3 small squid

1 tablespoon extra-virgin olive oil

6 ounces shelled cooked shrimp

CAPER DRESSING:

⅓ cup extra-virgin olive oil

2 tablespoons lemon juice

1 tablespoon chopped fresh parsley

1 clove garlic, finely chopped

1 tablespoon capers, drained

salt and pepper

parsley and lemon wedges, to garnish, if desired

Put mussels into a large saucepan with a cupful of water. Cover, cook over high heat for 5 minutes until mussles open. Remove from heat, discard any which remain closed. Allow to cool slightly.

Remove mussels from shells. Prepare clams in the same way, discarding any that remain closed.

To prepare squid, pull off tentacles and remove transparent bone in body. Remove any skin, then cut tubes into thin slices. Cut off tentacles just in front of eyes and set aside.

Heat oil in a heavy-based skillet. Add squid rings and tentacles and sauté for about 2 minutes until opaque. Turn into a bowl and add other shellfish.

To make dressing, mix ingredients together in a bowl or screwtop jar. Pour over fish and refrigerate for 2 hours.

Serve garnished with parsley and lemon wedges, if desired.

Serves 4.

CAPONATA

2 eggplants

salt

½ cup olive oil

1 small onion, chopped

4 sticks celery, chopped

14-ounce can chopped tomatoes

2-3 tablespoons red wine vinegar

1 tablespoon sugar

1 tablespoon capers, drained

12 green olives, pitted and chopped

1 tablespoon pine nuts, lightly toasted

salt and pepper

parsley sprigs, to garnish

Cut eggplants into small cubes, put into a colander. Sprinkle with salt and set aside to drain for 1 hour.

Meanwhile, heat 2 tablespoons oil in a saucepan, add onion and cook over medium heat for 5 minutes until soft. Add celery and continue to cook for 3 minutes. Stir in tomatoes and juice and simmer, uncovered, for 5 minutes. Add vinegar and sugar and simmer for a further 15 minutes.

Rinse eggplants and dry on paper towels. Heat remaining oil in a large skillet and cook eggplants, stirring, until tender and golden. Transfer with slotted spoon to tomato sauce. Add capers, olives and pine nuts and season with salt and pepper. Continue to simmer for 2-3 minutes.

Spoon into a serving dish and cool. Serve garnished with parsley.

Serves 6.

Note: This dish tastes better if left in the refrigerator for 24 hours to allow flavors to mingle.

Variation: For a more substantial dish, garnish with flaked tuna fish.

TOMATO & MOZZARELLA SALAD

2 beef tomatoes
6 ounces mozzarella cheese, sliced
1 small purple onion, thinly sliced
salt and pepper
¼ cup extra-virgin olive oil
1 tablespoon fresh basil leaves
1 tablespoon pine nuts

Slice the tomatoes and arrange with slices of cheese on 4 plates. Arrange onion rings on top. Season with salt and pepper, then drizzle oil over the top.

Scatter over the basil and pine nuts and serve at once.

Serves 4.

SPINACH & BACON SALAD

4 ounces young spinach leaves, washed and trimmed
2 ounces button mushrooms, sliced
3 thick slices bread, crusts removed
¼ cup sunflower oil
1 clove garlic, crushed
6 ounces bacon slices, chopped
2 tablespoons white wine vinegar
pepper

Shred spinach and put into a salad bowl with the mushrooms.

Cut bread into small squares. Heat oil in a skillet, add bread and garlic and fry until golden. Remove with a slotted spoon and drain on paper towels. Wipe out pan with paper towels, then add bacon and cook for about 5 minutes until crisp and golden.

Pour bacon and any fat over spinach. Add vinegar to pan with a few grinds of pepper, bring to a boil, then immediately pour over salad and toss. Scatter over the croutons and serve at once.

Serves 6.

SMOKED CHICKEN EXOTICA

3 smoked chicken breasts fillets, skinned

1 star fruit (carambola), sliced and seeds removed

1 papaya, peeled, seeded and sliced

2 fresh figs, quartered

½ mango, peeled and diced

1 tablespoon chopped candied ginger, to garnish

MANGO DRESSING:

½ mango, peeled

¼ cup sunflower oil

1 tablespoon sherry vinegar

pinch apple pie spice

Slice chicken and arrange on 4 plates with slices of star fruit, papaya, figs and diced mango.

To make the dressing, put ingredients into a blender and work until smooth. Drizzle over salads or place in the centers. Garnish with ginger.

Serves 4.

CHICKEN LIVER TIÈDE

6 ounces potato

6 ounces broccoli flowerets

2 small zucchini, sliced

8 ounces chicken livers, washed

¼ cup virgin olive oil

salt and pepper

2 tablespoons sherry vinegar

2 shallots, thinly sliced, to garnish

Cut the potato into ¼-inch matchsticks. Put into a saucepan of water, bring to a boil and cook for 3 minutes. Add broccoli and cook for 2 minutes. Add zucchini to pan and simmer a further 1 minute. Drain vegetables in a colander.

Cut membranes from chicken livers, then dry livers on paper towels. Heat oil in a skillet, add livers and season with salt and pepper. Cook for 5 minutes, stirring constantly; they should be soft and pink inside. Remove from the pan with slotted spoon.

Divide vegetables between 4 plates, slice the livers and scatter over vegetables.

Add vinegar to pan, warm quickly, then pour over the salads. Scatter over slices of shallot and serve at once.

Serves 4.

SOLE WITH CAPERS

2 sole fillets, each weighing about 8 ounces, skinned
1/3 cup dry white wine
2 heads endive, chopped
1 bunch watercress, trimmed
2 teaspoons capers
MARINADE:
1 lemon
1/4 cup virgin oil
2 tablespoons lemon juice
1 tablespoon chopped fresh parsley
1 shallot, finely chopped
salt and pepper

To prepare marinade, remove peel from lemon, using a zester. Squeeze the juice from the lemon and put into a bowl with other ingredients.

Cut fish fillets in half lengthwise, then across into thin strips. Place in a skillet with wine and poach for 2 minutes. Lift out of pan with a slot ted spoon, place in marinade and leave to marinate for 10 minutes.

Arrange endive and watercress on 4 plates. Remove fish from marinade and divide between plates.

Reduce poaching liquid to 4 tablespoons by boiling rapidly. Add capers and marinade, then warm together. Quickly pour over the salads and serve at once while the dressing is still hot.

Serves 4.

LOBSTER & ASPARAGUS SALAD

1 cooked lobster, weighing about 1½ pounds
8 ounces fresh asparagus, cut into 2-inch pieces
heart of 1 spring cabbage, weighing about 6 ounces, shredded
tarragon sprigs, to garnish
TARRAGON DRESSING:
3 tablespoons virgin olive oil
1 tablespoon tarragon vinegar
2 teaspoons chopped fresh tarragon, if desired
salt and pepper

To prepare lobster, remove large claws and pinchers. Crack open claws; remove meat, trying to keep it in chunks. Using point of a sharp knife, split lobster into 2 pieces from head to tail. Starting at tail, remove meat, discarding brown feathery gills. Remove liver to use in another recipe. Remove dark coral, if there is any, and reserve. Extract meat from body with a skewer. Slice the tail meat.

Cook asparagus in a steamer for 7 minutes. Add cabbage and steam for a further 2 minutes. Arrange vegetables and lobster meat on 4 plates.

To make the dressing, mix all the ingredients in a bowl or screw-top jar, then drizzle over the salads. Garnish with lobster coral and sprigs of tarragon. Serve at once.

Serves 4.

GOAT'S CHEESE SALAD

1 head radicchio
4 slices whole-wheat bread
two 4-ounce whole goat's cheeses
2 sticks celery, chopped
2 tablespoons walnut halves, chopped
celery leaves, to garnish
WALNUT GARLIC DRESSING:
3 tablespoons walnut oil
1 tablespoon red wine vinegar
1 clove garlic, crushed
salt and pepper

To make dressing, mix ingredients together in a bowl or screw-top jar.

Divide radicchio leaves and put into a bowl. Pour dressing onto the leaves and toss together, then arrange on 4 plates.

Toast bread; cut out 4 circles. Cut each cheese in half horizontally and trim off end crusts. Place a portion of cheese on each circle of toast, then place under medium-hot broiler for about 3-4 minutes until golden. Transfer to plates and scatter over the chopped celery and walnuts. Garnish with celery leaves and serve at once.

Serves 4.

SHRIMP WITH SNOW PEAS

12 raw jumbo shrimp
4 ounces snow peas, trimmed
3 tablespoons virgin olive oil
1 tablespoon finely shredded fresh ginger root
juice and grated peel of 1 lime
3 teaspoons soy sauce

Peel shrimp, leaving tail shells on. Make a small incision along spines. Remove black spinal cords from shrimp. Cook snow peas in boiling water for 1 minute, drain and arrange on 4 plates.

Heat the oil in a large skillet, add shrimp and ginger and cook gently for 5 minutes, turning them once.

Add lime juice, peel and soy sauce; cook for 1 minute. Arrange the shrimp on the snow peas, then pour over dressing. Serve at once.

Serves 4.

CALF'S LIVER BALSAMICO

| few batavia leaves |
| few lollo rosso leaves |
| 2 ounces mâche |
| ¼ cup extra-virgin olive oil |
| 2 large slices calf's liver, weighing 8 ounces, cut into ribbons |
| 1 tablespoon shredded fresh sage leaves |
| 2 tablespoons balsamico vinegar |
| salt and pepper |
| pine nuts, to garnish |

Tear salad leaves into smaller pieces and arrange on 4 plates.

Heat oil in a skillet, add liver and sage and cook for 2-3 minutes, stirring constantly. Remove with a slotted spoon and divide between the plates.

Pour vinegar into pan, season with salt and pepper and warm through. Spoon over the salads and serve garnished with pine nuts.

Serves 4.

TARAMASALATA

| 4 ounces smoked cod's roe |
| 1 cup dry bread crumbs |
| 2 teaspoons lemon juice |
| 1 clove garlic, crushed |
| ½ teaspoon black pepper |
| ⅓ cup olive oil |
| ⅓ cup low-fat soft cheese |
| 6 ripe olives and parsley sprigs, to garnish |

Using a sharp knife, cut through cod's roe skin and scrape out all the roe into a food processor fitted with a metal blade. Mix together bread crumbs and ¼ cup cold water and add to food processor with lemon juice, garlic and pepper.

Process for several seconds until mixture is well blended. Alternatively, press cod's roe through a strainer and beat in remaining ingredients, except the garnish.

Add oil drop by drop, beating well or using food processor until all oil has been incorporated.

Beat in cheese until mixture is smooth and creamy, then spoon in to a dish. Cover with plastic wrap and chill until required.

Garnish with ripe olives and parsley sprigs, and serve with Melba toast, crackers or sticks of fresh vegetables.

Makes 1¼ cups.

Variation: To serve as a thinner dressing, add enough plain yogurt to make the consistency required and serve with avocados or asparagus spears.

Serves 4.

NECTARINES & PROSCIUTTO

mixed salad leaves
2 nectarines or peaches
4 ounces prosciutto
fresh raspberries, to garnish, if desired
RASPBERRY VINAIGRETTE:
3 tablespoons virgin olive oil
5 teaspoons sunflower oil
1 tablespoon raspberry vinegar

Divide salad leaves between 4 plates.

Slice nectarines, halve slices of proscuitto and wrap around the fruit. Arrange on the salad leaves.

To make the dressing, mix ingredients together in a bowl or screw-top jar. Drizzle over the salad, then serve garnished with fresh raspberries, if desired.

Serves 4.

AVOCADO & STRAWBERRIES

2 avocados
8 ounces strawberries, hulled
mint or strawberry leaves, to garnish
HONEY LEMON DRESSING:
2 tablespoons sunflower oil
2 teaspoons lemon juice
¼ teaspoon paprika
salt and pepper

To make the dressing, put all the ingredients in a bowl or screw-top jar and mix well. Set aside

Cut avocados in half, remove seeds and peel. Dice the flesh and put into a bowl. If strawberries are large, slice or halve them, then add to avocado. Pour over dressing and toss together.

Divide between 4 dishes and serve garnished with leaves.

Serves 4.

SHRIMPS WITH GRAPEFRUIT

2 ounces young spinach leaves

1 bunch watercress, trimmed

2 ruby grapefruit

6 ounces shelled cooked shrimp

2 teaspoons chopped fresh chervil, to garnish

GRAPEFRUIT YOGURT DRESSING:

2 tablespoons thick yogurt

2 tablespoons virgin olive oil

1 teaspoon clear honey

salt and pepper

Wash spinach, dry and tear leaves into smaller pieces. Mix with watercress, then divide between 4 individual serving dishes.

Cut rind and pith from grapefruit. Holding each one over a bowl to catch juice, remove segments. Arrange the segments over the salad, then scatter the shrimp over the top.

To make the dressing, mix all the ingredients together in a bowl with 2 tablespoons of the reserved grapefruit juice, then spoon over the salads. Serve garnished with chervil.

Serves 4.

MELON & TOMATO SALAD

1 small honeydew melon or 2 galia, cantaloupe or rock melons

12 ounces tomatoes, skinned

mint sprigs, to garnish

MINT DRESSING:

2 tablespoons sunflower oil

2 teaspoons sherry vinegar

1 tablespoon chopped fresh mint

pepper

Cut melon or melons in half, remove seeds, then cut the flesh into cubes (or balls using a melon baller) and place in a bowl.

Quarter the tomatoes, remove seeds and cut each wedge across into 4 pieces. Add to the melon.

To make the dressing, mix all the ingredients together in a bowl or screw-top jar. Pour over the salad and stir gently. Cover well and chill for flavors to mingle.

Remove from refrigerator 30 minutes before serving. Spoon into 4 dishes or, if using the smaller variety of melons, spoon salad into the shells. Serve garnished with sprigs of mint.

Serves 4.

TANGY POTTED CHEESE

1 cup finely grated sharpe cheddar cheese
¼ cup butter, softened
1 tablespoon port or sherry
4 scallions finely chopped
½ teaspoon caraway seeds
½-1 teaspoon whole-grain mustard
¼ teaspoon Worcestershire sauce
¼ cup coarsely chopped walnuts
sprig of parsley, to garnish

Put grated cheese into a bowl and add softened butter. Mix well together until soft.

Stir in port or sherry, scallions, caraway seeds, mustard and Worcestershire sauce and mix thoroughly until well combined.

Spoon mixture into a small dish, cover with chopped walnuts and press down lightly. Chill for at least 2 hours. Serve, garnished with parsley, with crackers or Melba toast. *Serves 4-6.*

Note: This spread will keep in the refrigerator for up to 5 days.

Variation: Add 1 teaspoon chopped fresh herbs and a few pinches cayenne pepper to taste.

GUACAMOLE

2 ripe avocados
1 tablespoon lemon juice
1 small clove garlic, if desired
1 small fresh green chili, seeded
1 shallot, finely chopped
1 tablespoon olive oil
few drops hot-pepper sauce
salt
slices of lemon and sprig of parsley, to garnish
tortilla chips, to serve

Cut avocados in half, remove seeds and scoop flesh onto a plate. Mash well.

Add lemon juice and garlic, if desired, and mix well. Very finely chop chili and add to mixture together with chopped shallot.

Stir in oil, hot-pepper sauce and salt and mix well together. Turn mixture into a serving bowl, garnish with slices of lemon and sprig of parsley and serve with tortilla chips.

Serves 4-6.

—BARBECUES—

MARINADES AND BASTES

RICH TOMATO BASTE

1 large red pepper, seeded and finely chopped
1 pound tomatoes, skinned and chopped
1 small onion, finely chopped
1 clove garlic, finely chopped
2/3 cup dry white wine
large rosemary sprig
2 tablespoons sunflower oil
salt and pepper

Put first six ingredients in a saucepan. Simmer, uncovered, until thickened; purée. Add oil and seasoning.

BRANDY MARINADE

1/4 cup brandy
2/3 cup dry white wine
2 tablespoons olive oil
2 ounces tiny button mushrooms, finely sliced
2 shallots, finely chopped
1 teaspoon fresh thyme leaves
4 bay leaves
1 small clove garlic, crushed
10 peppercorns, crushed
1 teaspoon salt

Combine ingredients in a covered container. Leave for 24 hours. Strain.

SWEET & SOUR MARINADE

grated peel and juice of 1 orange
2/3 cup clear honey
2/3 cup red wine vinegar
3 tablespoons soy sauce
3 tablespoons Worcestershire sauce
1 tablespoon sesame oil

Combine all ingredients in a saucepan. Bring to a boil, then simmer, uncovered, for 5 minutes until sauce reduces by about one-third.

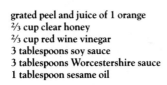

WARMLY SPICED BASTE

1/4 cup, plus 1 tablespoon dark soft brown sugar
2 tablespoons red wine vinegar
1/4 teaspoon ground cloves
1/4 teaspoon dry mustard
1 1/2 teaspoons ground allspice
3 teaspoons cornstarch
1 small eating apple, peeled, cored and finely chopped

Place ingredients in a saucepan. Add 7/8 cup water. Bring to a boil, stirring; simmer for 5 minutes or until thickened.

FIERY CHILI BASTE

2 tablespoons dark brown sugar
2/3 cup tomato ketchup
3/4 cup cider vinegar
2 tablespoons Worcestershire sauce
2 teaspoons chili powder
1/4 onion, finely chopped

Put sugar and 2/3 cup water in heavy-based saucepan. Stir until dissolved. Add remaining ingredients; bring to a boil. Simmer until reduced by about one-third.

CITRUS SHARP MARINADE

grated peel and juice of 4 limes
grated peel and juice of 1 lemon
2 teaspoons salt
6 tablespoons sunflower oil
12 white peppercorns, bruised

Mix all ingredients together in a bowl, cover and leave to infuse for 8 hours, or overnight. Strain marinade before using.

Note: All the recipes given here make 1 1/4 cups.

WHOLE FLOUNDER

four 1-pound flounder or plaice

STUFFING: 1 ½ cups soft bread crumbs
¼ cup butter, melted
2 teaspoons lemon juice
1 teaspoon grated lemon peel
2 teaspoons chopped fresh parsley
salt and pepper
1 ounce cooked shelled shrimps, thawed if frozen,
   finely chopped
1 egg, beaten
20 bay leaves
olive oil
16-20 grape leaves (from a package), soaked and
   drained
2 lemons and flat-leaved parsley sprigs, to garnish

Remove heads and clean fish. Make an incision to the bone through white skin to form a pocket and lift flesh away from bone. Mix together bread crumbs, butter, lemon juice and peel, parsley, salt and pepper to taste, shrimp and egg. Spoon into pockets. Insert 3-4 bay leaves over stuffing to hold in place. Brush fish all over with oil.

Line rectangular hinged grills with oiled grape leaves. Arrange remaining bay leaves over grape leaves and place fish between. Barbecue on rack over medium coals for 10-15 minutes on each side, basting occasionally with oil, until fish is cooked. Remove fish from baskets and discard charred leaves. Serve garnished with lemons and sprigs of flat-leaved parsley.

Serves 4.

RED MULLET WITH FENNEL

four 8-ounce red mullet
fennel leaves, to garnish

MARINADE: ¼ cup vegetable oil
1 teaspoon lemon juice
1 teaspoon fennel seeds
¼ teaspoon sea salt
¼ teaspoon pepper

Mix marinade ingredients together in a large shallow dish.

Scrape away hard scales, remove gills and fins and clean inside of fish, but do not remove liver. Rinse, drain and wipe dry with paper towel. Score through the skin twice on each side. Put fish in marinade and leave for 1 hour, basting occasionally.

Drain fish and lay on a wire rack over hot coals and barbecue for 6-8 minutes on each side, basting occasionally with marinade to prevent sticking and encourage browning. Garnish with fennel leaves.

Serves 4.

Note: To speed up cooking a greased tray may be inverted over fish.

LOUISIANA ANGELS

LUXURY GINGER SHRIMP

9 slices streaky bacon
18 button mushrooms
½ cup butter
2 tablespoons lemon juice
3 tablespoons chopped fresh parsley
pinch of cayenne pepper
18 fresh oysters, shelled
cornstarch for dusting
6 slices crustless toast, cut into fingers

1½ pounds jumbo shrimp
marjoram sprigs and lemon slices, to garnish

MARINADE: ⅔ cup vegetable oil
finely grated peel and juice of 1 small lemon
6 tablespoons soy sauce
1 clove garlic, crushed
1 teaspoon finely grated fresh ginger root
½ teaspoon dried marjoram

Stretch bacon slices slightly with back of a knife. Halve bacon crosswise. Lightly fry until opaque and still limp. Drain; set aside.

Mix together the marinade ingredients.

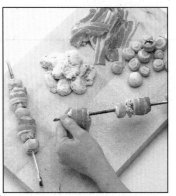

Cook mushrooms in saucepan of boiling water for 1 minute. Drain. To make maitre d'hôtel butter, melt butter in a pan. Remove from heat and stir in lemon juice, parsley and cayenne pepper. Keep warm. Dust oysters with cornstarch. Wrap bacon slices around oysters and alternately with mushrooms, thread on to 4-6 skewers. (Try to spear through "eyes" of oysters to keep them in position.)

Rinse shrimp well. Mix with marinade and leave in a cool place for 2 hours. Baste occasionally.

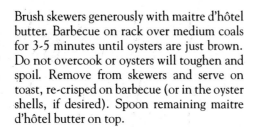

Brush skewers generously with maitre d'hôtel butter. Barbecue on rack over medium coals for 3-5 minutes until oysters are just brown. Do not overcook or oysters will toughen and spoil. Remove from skewers and serve on toast, re-crisped on barbecue (or in the oyster shells, if desired). Spoon remaining maitre d'hôtel butter on top.

Serves 6.

Thread crosswise onto skewers and barbecue over hot coals for 7-10 minutes, turning frequently until shrimp flesh is opaque. Remove from skewers and serve at once, garnished with marjoram sprigs and lemon slices.

Serves 6.

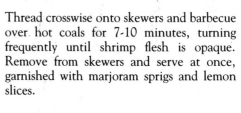

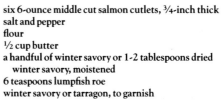

SIMPLY GRILLED LOBSTER

AROMATIC GRILLED SALMON

two 2-pound cooked lobsters
½ cup butter, softened
2 teaspoons lemon juice
salt and pepper
lemon wedges and parsley sprigs, to garnish

On a chopping board and using a heavy sharp knife, split lobsters in half by cutting lengthwise along line down the back and through the tail. Crack claws. Remove gills, grayish sac near head and black vein which runs lengthwise along tail.

Remove the coral and beat into half quantity of butter and set aside; melt remaining butter. Sprinkle lobster flesh with lemon juice and season lightly with salt and pepper. Brush generously with melted butter.

Barbecue lobster, flesh side uppermost, on an oiled rack over medium coals for about 5-10 minutes. Turn over and cook for 3-4 minutes until lobster meat is hot and browning slightly. Serve topped with coral butter. Garnish with lemon wedges and parsley sprigs.

Serves 4.

six 6-ounce middle cut salmon cutlets, ¾-inch thick
salt and pepper
flour
½ cup butter
a handful of winter savory or 1-2 tablespoons dried
   winter savory, moistened
6 teaspoons lumpfish roe
winter savory or tarragon, to garnish

Rinse salmon and pat dry on paper towels. Season to taste with salt and pepper; dip in flour and shake off surplus.

Melt butter and brush over salmon steaks. Place in a rectangular hinged basket. Sprinkle the winter savory over the coals when they are hot.

Barbecue fish on rack over hot coals for 4-5 minutes on each side, basting occasionally with melted butter. If the cutlets start to brown too quickly, reduce heat or move basket to side of barbecue. The cutlets are cooked when it is easy to move center bone. Serve sprinkled with lumpfish roe and garnish with winter savory or tarragon.

Serves 6.

SCALLOPS WITH TINDOORIS

2 pounds fresh or frozen scallops,
  thawed if frozen
12 tindooris (see Note)
2/3 cup olive oil
1 tablespoon lemon juice
1 tablespoon lime juice
1/4 teaspoon lemon pepper
1/4 teaspoon onion salt
lemon and lime slices, to garnish

Remove any dark veins, then rinse scallops and pat dry with paper towels. Rinse tindooris and halve lengthwise. Add to a saucepan of fast boiling water and cook for 1 minute. Drain and leave to cool.

Combine remaining ingredients, except garnish, in a large bowl. Put scallops into mixture and leave for 45 minutes – 1 hour, stirring occasionally. Add tindooris during the last 15 minutes.

Thread scallops and tindooris onto oiled skewers and barbecue on rack over medium coals for 5-10 minutes, basting frequently with marinade. Scallops are cooked when opaque. Garnish with lemon and lime slices.

Serves 6-8.

Note: Tindooris are a vegetable the size of a gherkin with smooth dark green skin and a texture similar to zucchini. They are obtainable from most Asian stores and supermarkets stocking exotic vegetables.

SWORDFISH KABOBS

2 pounds swordfish, skinned and boned
juice of 2 lemons
2 onions, peeled
18 cherry tomatoes
2/3 cup olive oil
1/2 teaspoon garlic salt
1/2 teaspoon pepper
6-8 tablespoons finely snipped fresh chives
6-8 tablespoons finely chopped fresh parsley
lemon slices and parsley sprigs, to garnish

Cut fish into 1 1/2-inch cubes and marinate in half the lemon juice for 1 hour, turning once.

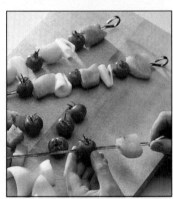

Halve onions and remove centers, leaving a three-layer wall. Separate layers, cutting each in half and curve to form a cone. Alternately thread fish cubes, onion cones and whole tomatoes onto skewers. Beat together oil, garlic salt, pepper and remaining lemon juice and brush over kabobs.

Barbecue on rack over medium coals for 10-15 minutes, turning frequently and brushing with oil baste. Mix together chives and parsley and spread on a chopping board. Roll hot kabobs in herb mixture before serving. Serve garnished with lemon slices and parsley.

Serves 6.

MACKEREL WITH RHUBARB SAUCE

6 fresh mackerel
salt and pepper
salad oil for brushing

SAUCE: 8 ounces trimmed rhubarb
1 teaspoon lemon juice
4 tablespoons sweet cider
3 tablespoons demerara sugar
¼ teaspoon grated nutmeg

Clean and gut mackerel, remove and discard heads. Season insides with salt and pepper to taste. Brush all over with oil.

Make long folded, double thickness foil strips about ½ inch wide. Wrap around fish, placing one near the top and the other in the center. Folding open ends twice to achieve a snug fit, at the same time form a flat loop to enable the fish to be handled easily.

Combine sauce ingredients in a heavy-based saucepan. Cover and cook gently, shaking pan occasionally until rhubarb is very soft. Purée in a blender and return to pan. Cover and keep hot. Brushing frequently with oil, barbecue the mackerel on a rack over medium coals for 7-10 minutes on each side until juices run clear when pricked deeply with a skewer. Use foil loops to help turn fish carefully. Serve with hot rhubarb sauce.

Serves 6.

PINK GRAPEFRUIT TROUT

6 small brown trout
4 pink grapefruit
1 ¼ cups dry white wine
4 scallions, trimmed and finely sliced
16 black peppercorns, lightly crushed
2 tablespoons heavy cream
⅓ cup butter
salt

Clean and gut the fish, removing the heads, if desired. Place each fish on oiled, double thickness foil, large enough for loose wrapping.

Thinly pare peel from 1 grapefruit and shred finely. Place shredded peel in a small saucepan. Cover with cold water, bring to a boil, then continue cooking for 3-4 minutes to soften. Drain and set aside. Remove pith, membranes and any seeds from pared grapefruit and segment flesh. Set aside for garnish. Grate peel and squeeze juice from remaining 3 grapefruit and put in a medium saucepan. Add wine, scallions and peppercorns. Simmer for 10-15 minutes until about ⅔ cup of liquid remains.

Remove from heat, stir in cream and butter; stir until butter melts, then strain into a jug. Season with salt to taste and mix in softened peel. Pour a little sauce over each fish and fold up foil, leaving a 1 inch space over fish for steam to circulate. Barbecue on rack over hot coals for 20 minutes, but do not turn the fish packages over. To serve, open foil, pour extra sauce over trout and garnish with reserved grapefruit segments.

Serves 4.

JUMBO SHRIMP

TARAMA SARDINES

juice of 1 large lemon
about ⅔ cup vegetable oil
18 raw jumbo shrimp, fresh or frozen, thawed if frozen
2 lemons and ¼ cucumber, to garnish

To prepare the garnish remove tops and bottoms from lemons and slice middle sections thinly. Using a canelle knife, remove strips of cucumber skin lengthwise. Thinly slice cucumber. Curve cucumber slices around lemon slices before threading on to wooden cocktail sticks.

6 fresh sardines
2 tablespoons lemon juice
pepper
3-4 tablespoons taramasalata
parsley sprigs, to garnish

Cut off and discard sardine heads and, using a small skewer or teaspoon, carefully clean out inside of each fish. Rinse and pat dry on paper towels.

Put lemon juice in one shallow dish and oil in another. Dip shrimp, 2 or 3 at a time, into lemon juice. Shake off surplus, then dip into the oil.

Brush inside sardines with lemon juice and season to taste with black pepper. Carefully fill cavities with the taramasalata.

Barbecue shrimp on a rack over hot coals for 10-12 minutes, brushing frequently with remaining oil. Serve hot, garnished with lemon and cucumber sticks, and have finger-bowls nearby.

Serves 6.

Note: Buy whole, unshelled jumbo shrimp for grilling. The gray-brown translucent appearance of these shrimp changes to orangey-pink when cooked.

Place sardines in a hinged rectangular basket and barbecue over hot coals for 3-4 minutes on each side. Arrange sardines in a spoke design on a round wooden platter. Garnish by inserting sprigs of parsley into the taramasalata.

Serves 6.

Variation: Use a small trout if sardines are not available and double the quantity of taramasalata.

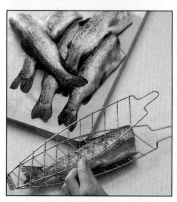

SEAFOOD KABOBS

12 ounces thick end monkfish, cut into bite-size pieces

3 flounder fillets, cut into thin strips

3 zucchini, cut into bite-size pieces

1 small yellow pepper, seeded and cut into bite-size pieces

12 large shrimp, shelled

MARINADE:

1/4 teaspoon powdered saffron

finely grated peel of 1 lime

3 tablespoons freshly squeezed lime juice

1 tablespoon clear honey

1 teaspoon green peppercorns, crushed

2 tablespoons white vermouth

1/3 cup grapeseed oil

1/2 teaspoon salt

1/2 teaspoon black pepper

6 fresh bay leaves

1 tablespoon chopped fresh dill

GARNISH:

bay leaves

6 lime wedges

dill sprigs

To make marinade, mix all the ingredients together. Add monkfish, flounder, zucchini, pepper and shrimp to marinade. Turn vegetables and fish carefully in marinade to coat evenly. Cover with plastic wrap and leave in a cool place for 1 hour. Meanwhile, soak 6 fine wooden skewers in cold water. Prepare barbecue or preheat broiled.

Thread alternate pieces of each fish, with zucchini and pepper in between, onto skewers with a bay leaf at the end of each. Cook for 5-8 minutes, turning only once and brushing with more marinade if necessary.

Arrange on a warmed serving dish and serve at once, garnished with fresh bay leaves, lime wedges and sprigs of dill.

Serves 6.

BARBECUED SARDINES

8 small sardines

MARINADE:

1/3 cup thick yogurt

1/2 teaspoon hot-pepper sauce

1/2 teaspoon cayenne pepper

1 tablepoon tomato paste

1/4 cup sherry

1/2 teaspoon salt

1/4 teaspoon black pepper

1 teaspoon sugar

4 teaspoons chopped fresh basil

2 teaspoons snipped fresh chives

2 teaspoons finely grated lemon peel

GARNISH:

herb sprigs

chive flowers, if desired

lemon wedges

Wash and clean sardines very gently as these fish need careful handling; remove heads if desired. Dry well on paper towels.

To make marinade, mix yogurt, hot-pepper sauce, cayenne, tomato paste, sherry, salt, pepper, sugar, basil, chives and lemon peel together, stirring until evenly blended. Pour into a large shallow dish.

Add sardines 1 at a time and turn gently in marinade to coat evenly. Cover with plastic wrap and leave in a cool place for 1-2 hours.

Meanwhile, prepare barbecue or preheat broiler. Arrange sardines on a fish or grill rack and cook for 5-6 minutes, turning only once, until crisp, brushing with more marinade if necessary.

Serve on a hot platter, garnished with fresh sprigs of herbs, chive flowers, if desired, and thin lemon wedges.

Serves 4.

Variation: If sardines are unavailable, use small trout or sprats.

TROUT IN SAFFRON FUMET

6 small rainbow trout
6 peppercorns
½ stick celery, coarsely chopped
1 parsley sprig
1 bay leaf
1 thyme sprig
3 thick slices carrot
1 shallot, coarsely chopped
¼ teaspoon salt
2 teaspoons white wine vinegar
½ cup dry white wine
½ teaspoon powdered saffron
¼-⅓ cup butter
celery leaves, to garnish

Remove heads and tails from fish; reserve.

Taking each fish in turn, slit along belly. Open flaps and place, open-edges down, on a work surface or board. Press with thumbs along backbone to flatten. Reverse fish and lift out backbone and reserve. Put fish heads, tails and backbones in a large saucepan, add 1¼ cups water and remaining ingredients, except butterflied fish, saffron, butter and celery leaves. Bring to a boil, then remove scum. Reduce heat, cover and simmer for 30 minutes.

Strain liquid into bowl through a fine nylon strainer. Return to saucepan, add saffron and boil vigorously, uncovered, until reduced to ¾ cup. Leave to cool. Place trout, flesh-side down, in large shallow dishes. Pour saffron fumet over fish and leave to marinate for 30 minutes. Remove from marinade. Melt butter and brush over fish. Barbecue in rectangular hinged baskets over hot coals for 2-3 minutes on each side. Garnish with celery leaves.

Serves 6.

HALIBUT STEAKS WITH DILL

4-6 sprigs fresh dill weed
8 tablespoons thick mayonnaise
salt and pepper
four 1-inch thick halibut steaks
4-6 tablespoons yellow cornmeal
fresh dill, to garnish

Strip the feathery leaves of dill weed away from stem. Mix leaves with mayonnaise and season to taste with salt and pepper.

Spread both sides of each fish steak with mayonnaise, then dip in cornmeal to lightly coat.

Barbecue halibut steaks on rack over hot coals for 10-15 minutes, turning once until fish is opaque and flaky when tested with tip of sharp knife. The surface of cooked steaks should be golden brown. Sometimes browning occurs before fish is cooked through, in which case reduce heat or move to edge of barbecue to finish cooking. Garnish with fresh dill.

Serves 4-6.

DANISH PATTIES

6 ounces trimmed pork fillet
6 ounces cooked ham
6 ounces Danish salami, skinned
parsley or cilantro sprigs, to garnish

DOUGH: 3 cups flour
pinch of salt
1 teaspoon baking powder
¼ cup vegetable shortening
⅔ cup milk

Using a food processor or mincer, finely chop all meats together.

Sift flour, salt and baking powder into a bowl. Cut in fat finely and mix to a soft dough with milk. Divide dough into 12 balls. On a lightly floured surface, flatten each ball into a 5-inch circle. Put an equal quantity of meat filling on the center of each circle. Dampen edges and seal by drawing them together. Press well to seal. Flatten slightly with the palm of the hand.

Thoroughly grease individual pieces of double thickness foil. Place one patty, seam-side down, on each piece of foil, flattening slightly with the palm of the hand. Wrap up securely. Cook over medium coals for about 10 minutes, turning foil packages over once during cooking. To test that the filling is completely cooked, insert a sharp-tipped knife into the center – no juices should escape. Garnish with sprigs of parsley or cilantro.

Makes 12.

PITA BURGERS

2 eggs, beaten
1 teaspoon turmeric
1 teaspoon cumin
¼ teaspoon cayenne pepper
2 cloves garlic, very finely chopped
2 pounds freshly ground lean beef
2 cups fresh bread crumbs
8 pitted green olives, chopped
6 pita breads, halved
lettuce and stuffed green olives, sliced, to garnish

In a large bowl, beat eggs with turmeric, cumin and cayenne pepper. Stir in garlic.

Mix meat, bread crumbs and chopped olives into the egg mixture and form into 12 burger shapes. Cook the burgers over hot coals for 8-10 minutes on each side.

When the burgers are nearly ready, warm the halved pita breads on the side of the rack. Open the cut sides of each pita and insert a burger. Serve wrapped in a paper napkin. Garnish with lettuce and sliced stuffed olives.

Makes 12.

BEEF & BACON SATAY

12 ounces lean beef
12 ounces unsmoked back bacon slices
1 onion, finely chopped
finely grated peel and juice of 2 lemons
4 tablespoons ground coriander
2 tablespoons ground cumin
¾ cup crunchy peanut butter
½ cup peanut oil
2 tablespoons clear honey
4 zucchini
scallion tassels, to garnish

Cut beef into 1-inch cubes. Put in a shallow dish. Trim bacon slices; halve lengthwise.

Stretch bacon slices on a work surface with a round-bladed knife drawn flat along each slice. Roll each up tightly along its length and add to dish with the cubed beef. Mix together the onion, lemon peel and juice, coriander, cumin, peanut butter, oil and honey. Pour over beef and bacon and marinate for at least 1 hour, basting occasionally.

Soak 18 bamboo skewers in water for 1 hour. Peel zucchini, cut in half lengthwise and then into ½-inch chunks. Alternately thread beef cubes, bacon rolls and zucchini chunks onto skewers. Barbecue on rack over hot coals for about 20 minutes, turning frequently. Serve with boiled rice and garnish with scallion tassels.

Makes 18.

LAMB KUMQUAT KABOBS

2 large oranges
1¼ pounds lean lamb
1½ cups cooked, short-grain rice
8-10 fresh mint leaves
salt and pepper
15 kumquats, rinsed, wiped and stems removed
olive oil for basting
mint sprigs, to garnish

SAUCE: 1 teaspoon arrowroot
¼ teaspoon sweet paprika
1 teaspoon maple syrup
2 teaspoons Cointreau

Squeeze the juice from oranges and make up to 1 cup with water.

Pare the orange peel and snip into pieces with kitchen scissors. Cube the lamb. Using a food processor, blend the peel, lamb, rice and mint to a smooth paste; season to taste with salt and pepper. This may need to be done in 2 batches. Divide the mixture into 20 equal portions, allowing 4 portions and 3 kumquats per skewer. Mold the meat paste into lozenge-shapes around 5 skewers, inter- spersing with kumquats.

Barbecue the kabobs on a rack over hot coals for 10-12 minutes, turning frequently and basting with olive oil. To make the sauce, smoothly blend reserved orange juice and arrowroot together in a small saucepan. Bring to a boil, stirring continuously until sauce thickens. Stir in the paprika, maple syrup and Cointreau. Keep sauce warm and use to coat kabobs just before serving. Garnish with mint sprigs.

Makes 5.

HAM & DAMSON SAUCE

JEWELED PORK CHOPS

four 5-ounce ham steaks

SAUCE: 1 pound damsons or other plums
4 tablespoons clear honey
4 tablespoons port
4 teaspoons sunflower oil

To prepare sauce, rinse damsons and cook gently in a tightly covered, heavy-based saucepan until fruit is very soft and broken up. Press fruit and juice through a nylon strainer over a bowl to extract pulp and juice. Discard skin and seeds.

Warm honey in a bowl over a pan of hot water and stir in the port, oil and damson pulp and juice. Leave bowl over hot water to keep honey liquified while barbecuing.

Snip edges of ham steaks with scissors to prevent them from curling up during grilling. Coat steaks thickly with damson sauce and grill over hot coals for about 5 minutes on each side, basting frequently with sauce.

Serves 4.

Note: Reserve any remaining sauce to coat latecomer's steaks to keep them moist.

3 shallots
½ small red pepper
½ small green pepper
⅓ cup shelled pistachio nuts
6 large pork chops, 1 inch thick
2 tablespoons walnut oil
2 tablespoons lemon juice
salt and pepper
12 tiny cocktail onions; 3 cocktail gherkins,
    thickly sliced and 6 cherries, pitted, to garnish

Peel and roughly chop shallots. Deseed and finely dice peppers. Halve nuts.

Put shallots, peppers and nuts in a bowl and cover with boiling water. Leave to stand for 10 minutes, then drain and discard liquid.

Using the tip of a sharp knife, make several small incisions into both sides of chops. Insert pieces of shallot, pepper and nut to stud surfaces. Mix together oil and lemon juice and use to brush over both sides of chops. Season to taste with salt and pepper. Barbecue on a rack over medium coals for 15-18 minutes on each side, basting occasionally with oil mixture. Garnish with cocktail onions, gherkins and cherries, threaded on to wooden cocktail sticks.

Serves 6.

WINE & PEPPER STEAKS

1¼ cups dry red wine
½ cup olive oil
2 tablespoons green peppercorns, ground
2 tablespoons coriander seeds
eight 1-inch thick sirloin steaks, trimmed
cilantro sprigs, to garnish
lightly salted, whipped cream, to serve, if desired

In a large bowl, mix together the wine, olive oil, ground peppercorns and coriander seeds.

Prick the steaks deeply, then immerse them in the marinade and leave for at least 2 hours.

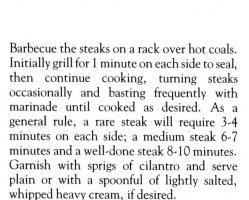

Barbecue the steaks on a rack over hot coals. Initially grill for 1 minute on each side to seal, then continue cooking, turning steaks occasionally and basting frequently with marinade until cooked as desired. As a general rule, a rare steak will require 3-4 minutes on each side; a medium steak 6-7 minutes and a well-done steak 8-10 minutes. Garnish with sprigs of cilantro and serve plain or with a spoonful of lightly salted, whipped heavy cream, if desired.

Serves 8.

SOUVLAKIA

1½ pounds lean lamb
1½ tablespoons sea salt
6 tablespoons chopped fresh oregano leaves
4 tablespoons olive oil
fresh bay leaves
1 large onion, finely chopped
6-8 cherry tomatoes, halved
1 small cucumber, peeled and sliced
2 lemons, cut into wedges
1¼ cups thick natural yogurt
oregano sprigs, to garnish

Cut the lamb into 1-inch cubes and toss in sea salt.

Mix 4 tablespoons chopped oregano leaves with olive oil. Skewer the lamb onto 4-5 skewers, interspersed with bay leaves. Leave generous gaps between the cubes to allow the heat to permeate more efficiently. Brush with oil mixture.

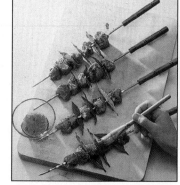

Barbecue the skewers on a rack over hot coals for 20 minutes, turning the skewers occasionally. Arrange the salad ingredients in sections on individual plates including a pool of yogurt at one side. Sprinkle with remaining oregano leaves. Remove the meat from the skewers using a fork and arrange in a line across the salad. Garnish with oregano.

Serves 4-5.

HOT DOGS WITH MUSTARD DIP

12-16 frankfurters
salt and pepper

DIP: 3 tablespoons dry mustard
1 cup light cream

To make the dip, blend the dry mustard and cream together in a bowl. Cover and leave in a cool place for 15 minutes, for the flavor to mature.

Prick the frankfurters and grill on an oiled rack over medium coals for 6-10 minutes, turning frequently. Season to taste with salt and pepper.

Wrap a twist of colored foil around one end of each frankfurter to make it easier to hold and arrange on a platter with a bowl of dip in the center. If preferred, cooked frankfurters can be coated with dip and inserted into long soft hot-dog rolls.

Makes 12-16.

ORIENTAL SPARE RIBS

6 pounds lean pork spare ribs
shredded scallions, to garnish

SAUCE: ½ cup hoisin sauce
½ cup miso paste
1¼ cups tomato paste
1½ teaspoons ground ginger
1½ teaspoons Chinese five-spice powder
1 cup dark brown sugar
3 cloves garlic, crushed
1 teaspoon salt
2 tablespoons saki (rice wine) or dry sherry

Separate the ribs and trim away most of the fat.

In a bowl, combine sauce ingredients and spread all over the ribs. Put the sauced ribs in a large shallow dish. Cover and leave in the refrigerator for at least 4 hours, or preferably overnight.

Place a drip pan in medium hot coals and barbecue ribs on a rack above the pan for 45-60 minutes, turning occasionally and basting with sauce. Heat any remaining sauce gently and serve separately. Garnish ribs with a shredded scallion.

Serves 8.

Note: Offer guests warmed damp cloths or packages of finger wipes.

PORKIES WITH CREAMY DIP

8-12 low-fat, thick pork or beef link sausages
oil for brushing

CREAMY DIP: 3 tablespoons grated horseradish
¼ cup cream cheese
2 tablespoons lemon juice
½ teaspoon sugar
½ teaspoon salt
⅔ cup thick soured cream

To make dip, blend horseradish, cream cheese, lemon juice, sugar and salt together. Gradually stir in thick soured cream. Cover and chill until required.

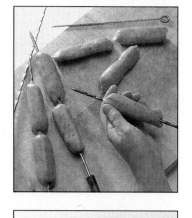

Prick sausages and thread onto skewers. Brush with oil. Barbecue on a rack over medium coals for 12-15 minutes until cooked through, turning frequently.

Arrange hot sausages in a circle on a wooden platter and place the prepared dip in the center. Serve with salads.

Serves 8-12.

VERMONT PORK CHOPS

4 pork chops, 1-inch thick
8-12 shelled pecans, dipped in maple syrup, and
    scallion tassels, to garnish

MARINADE: 4 scallions, trimmed and finely sliced
2 cloves garlic, very finely chopped
4 tablespoons maple syrup
4 teaspoons tomato ketchup
1 cup unsweetened apple juice
large pinch chili powder
large pinch ground cinnamon
large pinch pepper
1 teaspoon salt

Trim any surplus fat and pierce the chops on both sides.

Combine the marinade ingredients in a large shallow dish, stirring briskly with a fork to thoroughly blend in the tomato ketchup. Add the chops, turning them over to coat both sides. Cover and refrigerate for at least 2 hours, turning the chops over once or twice during this time.

Barbecue the chops on a rack over medium coals for 15-20 minutes on each side, basting frequently with the marinade. Just before serving, spoon the remaining marinade over the chops, evenly distributing any scallions that may still be in the bottom of the dish. Top each chop with 2 or 3 pecans and garnish with scallion tassels. Serve with roast sweet potatoes.

Serves 4.

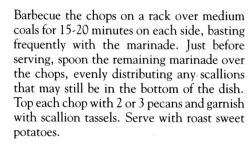

DRUNKEN ROAST PORK

3 pound pork joint, boned and rolled
2 tablespoons butter
1 large onion, chopped
2 carrots, thinly sliced
2 sticks celery, finely sliced
1 large leek, washed and sliced
⅔ cup medium red wine
1 tablespoon fresh thyme leaves
2 teaspoons fresh tarragon leaves
salt and pepper
2 tablespoons dry sherry
few thyme sprigs
2 tablespoons brandy
thyme and tarragon sprigs, to garnish

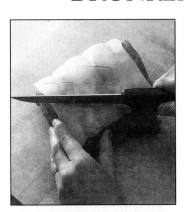

Score skin of joint; secure with string.

Place pork on a rack in a covered barbecue, and roast over low coals for about 2 hours. Unless using a spit, turn joint every 15 minutes to ensure even cooking. While roast is cooking, prepare sauce. Melt butter in a medium saucepan and gently fry onion until brown. Add carrots, celery, leek, wine and herbs. Cover and simmer, stirring occasionally, until vegetables are very soft. Pass through a strainer or purée mixture. Return to pan and season to taste with salt and pepper. Stir in sherry.

When the joint is thoroughly cooked in the center (and registers a temperature of 170F on a meat thermometer), pierce meat in several places and insert sprigs of fresh thyme. Place on a hot flameproof serving platter. Pour brandy into a metal ladle and heat gently over barbecue for a few seconds until warm. Pour over joint and immediately ignite. Spoon brandied juice into reheated sauce. Serve joint sliced, with a little sauce to side of each portion. Garnish.

Serves 6-8.

BEEF IN TAHINI PASTE

1¼ pounds beef tenderloin
4 tablespoons tahini (sesame seed paste)
¼ cup sesame oil
½ teaspoon garlic salt
1 tablespoon lemon juice
8 scallions, finely chopped
pepper
3 tablespoons sesame seeds, toasted
scallions tassels, to garnish

Slice beef across the grain into 20-25 thin slices.

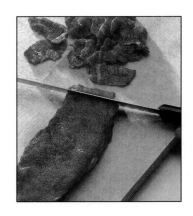

In a bowl, combine tahini, sesame oil, garlic salt, lemon juice and onions; season to taste with pepper. Using tongs, dip the beef slivers, one at a time, into the tahini baste, then spread them out on a board or tray. Cover with plastic wrap or foil and leave for at least 1 hour for the flavors to impregnate the meat. Reserve the tahini baste.

Prepare a hot barbecue grill and press the meat slices onto the rack. Using barbecue tongs, turn the slices over after 30 seconds and brush with the remaining baste. Grill for a further 1-1½ minutes. Arrange on a hot platter and sprinkle with toasted sesame seeds. Garnish with scallion tassels.

Serves 6.

CALF'S LIVER KABOBS

2 pounds calf's liver
6 tablespoons red wine
6 tablespoons sunflower oil
1 tablespoon Dijon mustard
½ teaspoon onion salt
½ teaspoon pepper
12 ounces small mushrooms
fresh herbs, to garnish, if desired

Trim the liver and cut into 1½-inch chunks.

In a large bowl, combine wine, oil, mustard, onion salt and pepper. Add liver and mushrooms. Mix thoroughly to coat. Marinate in the refrigerator for at least 1 hour, turning occasionally.

Thread the chunks of liver and mushrooms onto skewers. Barbecue on the rack over hot coals for 10-15 minutes, turning frequently and basting with marinade. Do not overcook or liver will become dry and tough. Garnish with fresh herbs, if desired. Serve with buttered egg noodles.

Serves 6-8.

MEXICAN MUFFINS

four 3-ounce sirloin steaks, ½-inch thick
1 large or 2 small ripe but firm avocados
2 teaspoons fresh lemon juice
2 ounces Mycella cheese, crumbled
2 English muffins
cayenne pepper

Grill the steaks on an oiled rack over hot coals according to desired doneness.

While the steaks are cooking, halve the avocado and remove seed. Scoop out flesh and, using a stainless steel fork, mash with the lemon juice and cheese. Split the English muffins in half and toast on both sides on the barbecue rack.

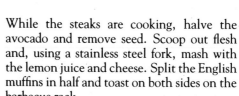

When the steaks are cooked spread with half the avocado mixture, cover with toasted muffin halves, then invert on to hot serving plates so that the muffins form a base. Top with a dollop of remaining avocado mixture and sprinkle with cayenne pepper.

Serves 4.

Note: The avocado mixture should not be prepared in advance or it will discolor.

LAMB & CHEESE SAUCE

12 ounces ground lamb
1 egg, beaten
1 teaspoon dried rosemary
½ cup fresh white bread crumbs
1 small red pepper, cored, seeded and minced
1 teaspoon hot-pepper sauce
½ teaspoon onion salt
½ teaspoon pepper

SAUCE: 1½ teaspoons butter
1 tablespoon flour
½ cup milk
1 egg yolk
⅓ cup thick soured cream
2 ounces feta cheese, crumbled

Thoroughly mix the lamb, egg, rosemary, bread crumbs, minced pepper, hot-pepper sauce, onion salt and pepper. Shape the mixture into about 16 rectangular fingers and refrigerate for 30 minutes. Meanwhile, make sauce. Melt butter in a small saucepan, stir in the flour, remove from the heat and thoroughly blend in the milk. Cook over moderate heat, stirring continuously until sauce thickens to the consistency of thin cream. Remove pan from heat. Blend the egg yolk with the cream and pour into pan. Mix in cheese. Cook gently until cheese has just melted.

Barbecue the lamb fingers on an oiled rack over hot coals for 5-6 minutes on each side, reducing the heat if they become too brown. Arrange 4 neat fingers in a fan shape on each plate and spoon some sauce over the tips, allowing it to form a pool.

Serves 4.

Note: Garnish the lamb fingers with red pepper rings or sprigs of rosemary, if desired.

BACON LATTICE STEAKS

four 7½-ounce sirloin steaks, 1 inch thick
4 lean slices smoked bacon
pepper
¼ cup olive oil
1 cup coleslaw
parsley sprigs, to garnish, if desired

Make 3 deep diagonal slashes lengthwise and 3 slashes crosswise on each side of the steaks but do not cut right through.

Cut the bacon into thin strips and insert into the slashes to form a lattice. Press with the palm of the hand. Season the steaks with pepper and brush all over with oil.

Barbecue the steaks on a rack over hot coals, turning immediately the underside is sealed (this is important to ensure juicy steaks). Turn the steaks over frequently during cooking until desired doneness is reached, about 5 minutes on each side for rare. Serve with coleslaw. Garnish with sprigs of parsley, if desired.

Serves 4.

LAMB CHOPS TAMARIND

3 tablespoons butter
1 onion, finely chopped
2 tablespoons tamarind concentrate (See note)
2 tablespoons tomato paste
1-inch piece fresh ginger root, finely grated
2 teaspoons dark soft brown sugar
2 tablespoons olive oil
grated peel and juice of 1 large orange
6 double loin lamb chops
orange segments, orange peel and parsley sprigs, to
    garnish

Melt the butter in a saucepan and cook onion until transparent.

Add tamarind concentrate, tomato paste, ginger root, sugar, oil and orange peel and juice and simmer gently, uncovered, for 7-8 minutes until reduced by a quarter. Leave to cool. Coat the chops thoroughly in the sauce, then cover and refrigerate overnight.

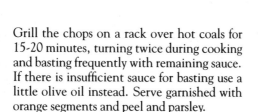

Grill the chops on a rack over hot coals for 15-20 minutes, turning twice during cooking and basting frequently with remaining sauce. If there is insufficient sauce for basting use a little olive oil instead. Serve garnished with orange segments and peel and parsley.

Serves 6.

Note: Tamarind concentrate is popular in Southeast Asian cooking. It has a sour taste and is dark brown. Look for it in Asian supermarkets.

BLUEBERRY VENISON

6 venison steaks
grated peel and juice of 2 oranges
juice of 1 lemon
3 tablespoons whiskey
½ cup olive oil
1 teaspoon rosemary leaves
3 bay leaves, crumbled
1 teaspoon celery salt
8 ounces blueberries
1 cup soft brown sugar
1 tablespoon lemon juice

Trim venison steaks and place on a chopping board. Flatten with a mallet or rolling pin.

Mix together orange peel and citrus juices, whiskey, oil, rosemary, bay leaves and celery salt in a large, shallow dish. Place venison steaks in marinade, turning over to coat both sides. Leave in refrigerator for 6-8 hours, basting occasionally. Remove stems from blueberries. In a heavy-based saucepan, combine sugar, remaining 1 tablespoon lemon juice and ⅔ cup water. Heat gently, stirring until sugar dissolves. Add blueberries and bring to a boil. Reduce heat and cook until pulpy. Keep warm.

Remove venison steaks from marinade and barbecue on an oiled rack over hot coals for about 10 seconds on each side to seal meat. Brush with marinade and continue cooking for 5-7 minutes on each side until tender. Serve with blueberry sauce.

Serves 6.

Note: Garnish each portion with a few bay leaves, blueberries and orange slices, if desired.

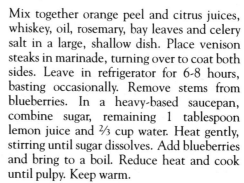

CHICKEN ST. LUCIA

²/₃ cup grated creamed coconut
1 teaspoon ground cumin
1 teaspoon ground cardamom
4 tablespoons mango chutney
¹/₂ cup corn oil
1¹/₂-2 teaspoons salt
4 teaspoons turmeric
four 10-12 ounce chicken quarters

Heat ¹/₄ cup water in a small saucepan, stir in the grated coconut and when well blended, remove from the heat. Stir in the cumin, cardamom and mango chutney. Spoon the mixture into a bowl, cover and set aside.

Mix together the oil, salt and turmeric and brush generously all over the chicken quarters. Barbecue the chicken quarters on a rack over medium coals for 12-15 minutes on each side, basting frequently with the remaining seasoned oil. Pierce through to the bone with a skewer to make sure that the juices are clear and the chicken is fully cooked.

Serve with a tiny pot of the sauce on the side of the plate.

Serves 4.

CRANBERRY BALLOTINE

2 pound oven-ready chicken
1 onion, chopped
2 tablespoons vegetable oil
¹/₂ cup long-grain rice
⁷/₈ cup chicken stock
¹/₂ cup raisins
grated peel and juice of 1 lemon
salt and pepper
1 egg, beaten
¹/₃ cup cooked and drained cranberries
¹/₂ teaspoon sugar

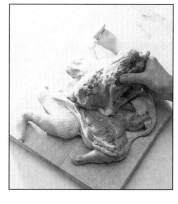

Remove chicken wings at second joint and reserve. Loosen skin at neck, cut around wishbone and remove.

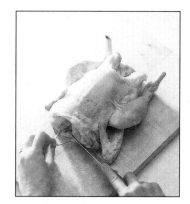

Cut through skin and flesh along backbone. Follow contour of carcass carefully; cut flesh away from bone without damaging skin. Sever shoulder joint, ease carcass out from skin and flesh and push back skin from thighs. Cut away flesh and turn inside out to free bone from skin. Repeat for wing bones. Spread skin out and cover evenly with flesh. Use carcass and bones to make stock. Fry onion in oil until soft. Add rice, hot stock, raisins, lemon peel and juice. Cover; simmer for 20 minutes until stock is absorbed.

Season rice mixture to taste with salt and pepper. Cool, then beat in egg. Spread over flesh side of chicken, leaving a ³/₄-inch border. Sweeten cranberries; spoon lengthwise along center of rice. Re-shape and sew chicken. Roast on rack over low coals, in a covered barbecue, for 1-1¹/₄ hours until chicken is dark golden brown. Leave to stand for 10-15 minutes before carving.

Serves 4.

CHICKEN TERIYAKI

1½ pounds chicken breasts fillets, skinned
three 8-ounce cans water chestnuts
¼ cup dry sherry
¼ cup medium-dry white wine
¼ cup shoyu sauce
2 cloves garlic, crushed
sunflower oil for brushing
shredded lettuce, onion rings, parsley sprigs and
    paprika, to garnish, if desired

Cut the chicken into 1-inch cubes. Drain water chestnuts and mix together in a dish. In a small bowl, mix together sherry, wine, shoyu sauce and garlic.

Pour the liquid mixture over chicken and water chestnuts, cover and leave to marinate for 30-60 minutes, stirring occasionally. Using a slotted spoon, remove chicken cubes and water chestnuts from marinade. Thread pieces of chicken and water chestnuts alternately onto 8 long skewers. Reserve any remaining marinade.

Brush chicken and chestnuts with oil and barbecue on a rack over hot coals for about 10 minutes, turning frequently and basting with reserved marinade and oil. Arrange shredded lettuce on a large platter and place skewers in a criss-cross pattern on top. Garnish with raw onion rings, parsley and a sprinkling of paprika, if desired.

Serves 8.

CHICKEN LIVER KABOBS

1¼ pounds chicken livers, rinsed and trimmed
¼ cup sunflower oil
1 onion, finely chopped
1 clove garlic, crushed
¼ cup dry red wine
½ teaspoon hot-pepper sauce
1½ teaspoons dark soft brown sugar
12 black peppercorns
salt
18 canned water chestnuts
1 large red pepper, cored, seeded and sliced into rings

Halve or quarter chicken livers, depending on size.

Heat oil in a small saucepan and gently fry onion until soft. Add garlic, wine, hot-pepper sauce, sugar and peppercorns and season with salt to taste. Bring to a boil, add prepared livers and simmer for 1 minute to firm liver. Remove from heat and leave to marinate for 2 hours.

Using a slotted spoon, remove livers from marinade. Thread alternately onto 6 skewers, with the water chestnuts. Discard the peppercorns from marinade. Barbecue on rack over hot coals for 6-8 minutes, turning frequently and basting occasionally with marinade. Serve with red pepper rings, dressed with remaining marinade.

Serves 6.

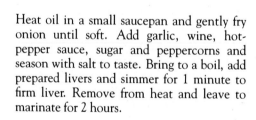

CHICKEN SATAY

2 tablespoons peanut oil
1 large onion, finely chopped
3 cloves garlic, finely chopped
7 ounces creamed coconut
2 cups hot water
2 tablespoons lemon juice
2 teaspoons salt
1 teaspoon ground cardamom
½ teaspoon ground ginger
2 teaspoons turmeric
⅔ cup unsalted peanuts, roasted,
    skinned and finely ground
1½ pounds chicken breast fillets, skinned and cut into
    1-inch cubes
lemon slices or wedges and cilantro sprigs, to garnish

Heat oil and gently fry onion and garlic until soft. In a large bowl, blend coconut with hot water and add lemon juice, salt, cardamom, ginger, turmeric and peanuts. Add cooked onion and garlic, including any oil left in pan. Add cubed chicken and stir well. Cover bowl, put in refrigerator and leave to marinate for 4 hours.

Remove cubed chicken from marinade and thread onto 8 skewers. Barbecue on rack over hot coals for 10-12 minutes, turning frequently and basting with remaining marinade. Serve garnished with lemon and cilantro.

Serves 8.

Note: This dish is delicious served with shrimp crackers which are obtainable from larger supermarkets, delicatessens, Chinese, Japanese and Asian food stores.

DEEP SOUTH DRUMSTICKS

12-16 chicken drumsticks
1-inch slice whole-wheat bread
6 tablespoons tomato paste
3 tablespoons full-bodied red wine
juice of ½ lemon
2 tablespoons Worcestershire sauce
2 tablespoons molasses
1 teaspoon salt
½ teaspoon pepper
1 teaspoon French mustard
½ teaspoon chili powder
1 teaspoon paprika
2 tablespoons oil
parsley sprigs, to garnish

Wash and dry drumsticks and set aside.

Remove the crusts, then dice the bread. Put in a large shallow dish, with all the remaining ingredients, except parsley. Stir with a fork until the bread is incorporated. (The mixture with be thick.) Put the drumsticks into the sauce, twisting at the bone end to coat evenly. Leave in a cool place for 1 hour, turning drumsticks occasionally.

Wrap drumsticks individually in oiled, single thickness foil. Barbecue on a rack over medium hot coals for 30-40 minutes, turning the packages from time to time. Test 1 drumstick for doneness by pricking with a skewer – the juices should run clear and flesh touching the bone be fully cooked. Garnish with parsley and serve in the foil pockets with baby corn.

Serves 12-16.

SPATCHCOCKED CHICKEN

POUSSIN AIOLI

two 1-pound oven-ready poussins or spring chickens
3 tablespoons butter
¾ teaspoon grated lemon peel
¾ teaspoon dry mustard
⅓ cup heavy cream
parsley sprigs, to garnish

On a wooden chopping board, and using poultry shears or a heavy, sharp-bladed knife, cut the birds through the backbone. With skin-sides uppermost, flatten each bird to 1-inch thickness using a mallet or rolling pin.

5 cloves garlic, peeled
2 egg yolks
½ cup olive oil
1 teaspoon lemon juice
salt and pepper
2 oven-ready poussins
lemon slices and parsley sprigs, to garnish

In a glass bowl, pound garlic to a pulp with a pestle. Gradually beat in egg yolks.

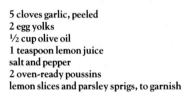

Soften butter and blend in the lemon peel, mustard and cream. Spread split chickens with half the mixture. Diagonally insert 2 long skewers through both thighs and breast, crossing them over in the center.

Beat oil into mixture drop by drop until it starts to thicken. Mix lemon juice with 1 teaspoon water and beat in alternate drops of juice and oil until well incorporated. Season to taste with salt and pepper.

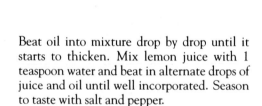

Barbecue on a rack over hot coals for 20 minutes, basting occasionally with remaining butter cream and turning once. Reduce heat and move birds to side of barbecue. Continue cooking for about 20 minutes, or until juices run clear when pricked with a skewer, turning once. Remove skewers and halve before serving, garnished with parsley sprigs.

Serves 4.

Loosen skin of poussins and, using a spoon handle, spread garlic mayonnaise close to the flesh. Brush mixture inside each cavity and also over outside of birds. Separately wrap each poussin in double thickness foil. Barbecue on rack over medium coals for 30 minutes. Remove poussins from foil, barbecue on rack for further 15-20 minutes, turning and basting occasionally. Serve poussins, whole or halved, garnished with lemon and parsley.

Serves 2-4.

SAUCY SPIT-ROAST DUCKLING

4½ pound oven-ready duck
salt and pepper
⅔ cup pineapple juice

SAUCE: 1 pound pitted black cherries
1 clove garlic, unskinned
⅔ cup port
1¾ cups well-flavored, strong beef stock
1 tablespoon potato flour
2 tablespoons butter
1 tablespoon red-currant jelly

Prick duck skin in several places. Season inside and out with salt and pepper. Sprinkle inside with a little pineapple juice.

To make sauce, put cherries, garlic, port and stock in a saucepan and poach until cherries are tender. Remove cherries with a slotted spoon and set aside. Discard garlic. Blend potato flour with 2 tablespoons cold water, stir into liquid in pan and bring to a boil, stirring continuously until thickened. Mix in butter, red-currant jelly and salt and pepper to taste. Add cherries and cook until hot. Reheat on side of barbecue when duck is cooked.

When the barbecue coals are hot move them toward side and place a roasting tin in center. This must be large enough to catch drips (which are considerable). Fix duck on to a spit or put in a roasting basket. Barbecue over medium heat for 2½-3 hours until well cooked. Foil tenting or covering with barbecue lid will hasten cooking. Do not open for 30 minutes, then baste every 10 minutes with pineapple juice. Pour away fat; mix juices into sauce and serve with duck.

Serves 6-8.

CHINESE DUCK

three 1-pound duck breast quarters
hoisin sauce
bunch scallions, trimmed and shredded

MARINADE: 2 teaspoons miso paste
⅓ cup dry sherry or saki
¼-½ teaspoon Chinese five-spice powder

CHINESE PANCAKES: 2 cups hard white flour
¾ cup boiling water
sesame oil

Deeply score the duck flesh through to the bone in a criss-cross fashion. Thoroughly blend the marinade ingredients together.

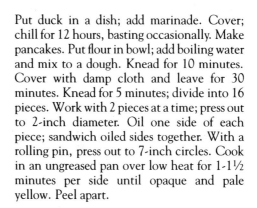

Put duck in a dish; add marinade. Cover; chill for 12 hours, basting occasionally. Make pancakes. Put flour in bowl; add boiling water and mix to a dough. Knead for 10 minutes. Cover with damp cloth and leave for 30 minutes. Knead for 5 minutes; divide into 16 pieces. Work with 2 pieces at a time; press out to 2-inch diameter. Oil one side of each piece; sandwich oiled sides together. With a rolling pin, press out to 7-inch circles. Cook in an ungreased pan over low heat for 1-1½ minutes per side until opaque and pale yellow. Peel apart.

Barbecue the duck quarters on a rack over low coals in a covered barbecue for about 1 hour, turning them over 3 times during cooking and basting with any remaining marinade. If using an unlidded barbecue, tent with foil and allow extra time. Shred the meat from the bone while duck is still hot. Serve a portion of shredded duck with 3 or 4 pancakes, a tiny dish of hoisin sauce and the onions. The pancakes are eaten spread with sauce and filled with duck and onions.

Serves 3-4.

GINGER & APRICOT CHICKEN

8-10 unboned chicken thighs
14½-ounce can apricot halves in natural juice
about 1 cup orange juice
1 tablespoon walnut oil
1 small slice onion, minced
1 teaspoon grated fresh ginger root
salt and pepper
16 red cherries, pitted

Deeply slash each chicken thigh to the bone in 2 or 3 places.

Remove the apricot halves from the juice, reserve 16 for garnish and mash the remainder. Make the juice up to 1½ cups with orange juice. Pour into a large bowl, add the oil, mashed apricots, onion and ginger and season to taste with salt and pepper. Mix in the chicken thighs, cover and leave in a cool place for 2 hours, stirring occasionally.

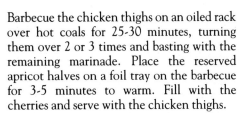

Barbecue the chicken thighs on an oiled rack over hot coals for 25-30 minutes, turning them over 2 or 3 times and basting with the remaining marinade. Place the reserved apricot halves on a foil tray on the barbecue for 3-5 minutes to warm. Fill with the cherries and serve with the chicken thighs.

Serves 4.

PIQUANT SPRING CHICKEN

2 spring chickens
1½ cups tomato juice
¼ cup Worcestershire sauce
2 teaspoons lemon juice
juice of ½ orange
salt and pepper
4 heads endive
knob of butter
1 orange, thinly sliced, to garnish

Halve the chickens so that each has a wing and a leg. Place cut-side up in a shallow dish.

Combine the tomato juice, Worcestershire sauce and citrus juices. Season generously with pepper. Pour over the chicken, cover and refrigerate for 12 hours, basting occasionally. Put the endive heads on individual pieces of double thickness foil. Dot with butter and season to taste with salt and pepper. Wrap tightly.

Barbecue the chickens on an oiled rack over medium coals for 30-40 minutes until well cooked, basting occasionally with the marinade. Cook endive parcels over or in medium coals during the final 10-12 minutes. Garnish the chicken halves with orange slices and serve with the endive.

Serves 4.

CAPERED NEW POTATOES

1 pound new potatoes
3 tablespoons capers
⅓ cup butter, softened
parsley sprigs, to garnish

Scrub potatoes well, then boil in their skins in salted water for 10 minutes. Drain and leave to cool slightly

Finely chop the capers and blend with butter. Make a deep slit in each potato and fill with caper butter.

Tightly wrap each potato in separate squares of single thickness foil and barbecue on rack over hot coals for 10-15 minutes. Garnish with sprigs of parsley.

Serves 4-6.

Note: These barbecued potatoes are also ideal as an accompaniment to plain broiled fish or poultry.

WHOLE TOMATOES IN WINE

8 firm tomatoes
8 teaspoons red wine
salt and pepper
watercress or lettuce leaves, to serve, if desired

Cut 8 large squares of double thickness foil. Cup each tomato in foil but do not completely enclose.

Pour over 1 teaspoon wine and season to taste with salt and pepper. Mold foil around tomatoes securely to prevent juices escaping.

Put packages on side of rack over medium coals and cook for about 10-15 minutes. Unwrap and transfer to serving plates, spooning wine-flavored juices over tomatoes. Serve on a bed of watercress or lettuce leaves, if desired.

Serves 8.

Note: The tomatoes are particularly delicious as an accompaniment to barbecued steaks or burgers which can be cooked at the same time.

HOT HOT ALOO

1 pound small new potatoes
12 teaspoons lime pickle
¼ cup vegetable oil
2 teaspoons tomato paste
2 teaspoons ground cardamom
2 tablespoons plain yogurt
lime slices, to garnish

Wash and scrub potatoes. Cook in salted water until tender but firm. Drain. Leave until cold, then thread onto 4-6 skewers.

Put lime pickle in a glass bowl and using kitchen scissors, cut up any large pieces of the pickle. Blend in oil, tomato paste, cardamom and yogurt.

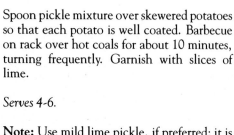

Spoon pickle mixture over skewered potatoes so that each potato is well coated. Barbecue on rack over hot coals for about 10 minutes, turning frequently. Garnish with slices of lime.

Serves 4-6.

Note: Use mild lime pickle, if preferred; it is very hot and spicy. Look for lime pickle at Asian supermarkets.

SWEET & SOUR EGGPLANTS

2 eggplants
3 tablespoons tarragon vinegar
3 tablespoons olive oil
1 small clove garlic, crushed
pinch of salt
½ teaspoon French mustard
1 tablespoon chopped fresh parsley
½ teaspoon dried marjoram
pinch of cayenne pepper
1 tablespoon sugar
marjoram sprigs, to garnish

Peel eggplants, cut in half, then slice and cut into ½-inch cubes.

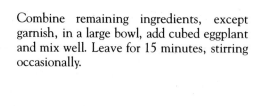

Combine remaining ingredients, except garnish, in a large bowl, add cubed eggplant and mix well. Leave for 15 minutes, stirring occasionally.

Thread onto 8 skewers and barbecue over hot coals for 15 minutes, turning occasionally. Garnish with sprigs of marjoram.

Serves 8.

Note: These are extremely good served with barbecued or broiled steaks or chops.

COUNTY MUSHROOMS

SPANISH CHAR-GRILLED ONIONS

12 open, flat mushrooms, each weighing about
  2 ounces
¾ cup virgin olive oil
¼ cup lemon juice
5 teaspoons grated fresh horseradish
¼ teaspoon salt
¼ teaspoon pepper
1 tablespoon chopped fresh parsley, to garnish

Wipe mushrooms and, if needed, cut stems to
½ inch long.

2 large Spanish or red onions
garlic salt
¼ cup heavy cream, half-whipped
1 tablespoon crushed black peppercorns
2 tablespoons butter
rosemary sprigs, to garnish

Peel onions and cut into ½-inch thick slices.
Do not separate into rings.

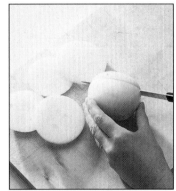

Thoroughly mix olive oil, lemon juice, grated
horseradish and salt and pepper in a large
shallow dish. Add mushrooms, spooning
liquid over to completely coat. Leave to stand
for at least 30 minutes, basting occasionally.

Season to taste with garlic salt. Brush one
side with heavy cream and sprinkle with
crushed peppercorns.

Barbecue on rack over hot coals for about 10
minutes, turning over and basting
occasionally. Garnish open sides of
mushrooms with chopped parsley.

Serves 6-12.

Barbecue in a tented, hinged wire basket and
cook cream-side up first. Barbecue over hot
coals for 5-8 minutes on each side until
beginning to "charcoal." Put dabs of butter
on surface of onion slices while first sides are
cooking. Serve peppered-sides up, garnished
with sprigs of rosemary.

Makes 8-10.

Note: Serve with meat dishes, or as an
appetizer.

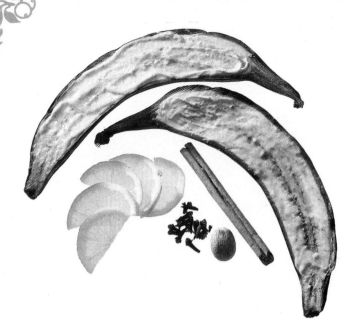

SINGED SPICED PLANTAINS

SAGE & CREAM BAKES

6 plantains or under-ripe bananas
2 tablespoons butter
2 tablespoons lemon juice
½ teaspoon quatre épices (see Note)
pinch of ground ginger
lemon slices, to garnish

Without peeling, barbecue the plantains or bananas over medium coals, turning them over until the skins blacken.

6 baking potatoes
vegetable oil
2 tablespoons white wine vinegar
1 bunch scallions, finely sliced
1 egg yolk
pinch of dry mustard
salt and pepper
1 teaspoon sage leaves, finely chopped
⅔ cup thick soured cream
fresh sage leaves, to garnish

Scrub potatoes and dry on paper towels. Prick deeply through skins and rub with oil.

Soften the butter, mix in the lemon juice, quatre épices and ginger.

Wrap potatoes separately in double thickness foil and bake in coals for 45 minutes-1 hour, turning occasionally until soft. Put vinegar in a small saucepan, add scallions and cook over low heat until vinegar has almost evaporated. Remove pan from heat. Beat together egg yolk, mustard and salt and pepper to taste and stir into scallions.

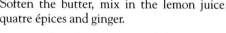

Slit the cooked plantains or bananas to separate into halves and spoon the spicy butter over the surface. Garnish with lemon slices.

Serves 6-12.

Note: Quatre épices is a spicy mixture of ground pepper, cloves, nutmeg and either cinnamon or ginger. It is obtainable from many delicatessens.

Singed Spiced Plantains are delicious served with chicken, ham or veal dishes.

Cook over very low heat for 1 minute, beating continuously until mixture thickens. Care must be taken not to overheat or sauce may curdle. Remove from heat; stir in chopped sage and cream. Cut a deep cross through foil into cooked potatoes and squeeze sides to open out. Spoon in a little sauce. Garnish with sage leaves.

Serves 6.

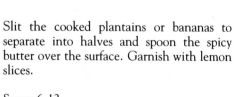

ZUCCHINI WITH HERBS

8-10 young firm zucchini, about 5 inches long
1 teaspoon lemon verbena leaves
4-5 fresh mint leaves
1 teaspoon marjoram leaves
2 bay leaves
½ teaspoon salt
2 tablespoons medium white wine
2 tablespoons lemon juice
¼ cup sunflower oil
lemon slices and fresh herbs, to garnish

Rinse and dry zucchini and pierce at either end and in one or two places along length. Finely chop herbs.

In a large bowl, mix together herbs, salt, wine, lemon juice and oil. Add zucchini, turning over to coat thoroughly. Cover and marinate for 4-5 hours, tossing occasionally.

Remove zucchini from marinade and barbecue on rack over hot coals for about 8-10 minutes until tender, but not soft, turning frequently and basting with remaining marinade. Serve skewered with wooden sticks. Garnish with lemon slices and fresh herbs.

Serves 8-10.

WALNUT APPLE CRESCENTS

2 small, red-skinned eating apples
⅓ cup shelled walnuts
1-ounce block dried dates
¼ cup apple juice
1 teaspoon grated orange peel
strips of orange peel, to garnish

Rinse and dry apples and remove cores, keeping apples whole. Cut each apple in half lengthwise. (Each half will have a tubular shaped hollow along center.)

Roughly chop walnuts and dates. Put apple juice and grated orange peel in a small saucepan. Add walnuts and dates, bring to a boil, then simmer for 2-3 minutes until liquid has been absorbed. Cool slightly, then fill apple hollows with mixture.

Wrap each apple half separately in double thickness foil. Barbecue on rack over hot coals for about 30 minutes, turning occasionally until apples are tender. Garnish with strips of orange peel.

Serves 4.

Note: Serve as an accompaniment to poultry or game.

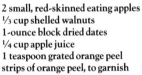

SKEWERED POTATO CRISPS

two 8-ounce baking potatoes
hot water
salt
¼ cup sunflower oil

Peel potatoes. Carefully cut into paper thin slices lengthwise, following the curve of the potato.

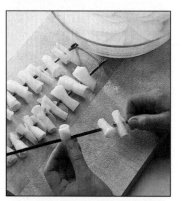

Immediately plunge potato slices into hot, salted water. Stir to separate, then leave for 3-4 minutes until pliable. Carefully coil each potato slice, then thread onto long skewers, leaving at least ½-inch space between each one.

Brush potato coils with oil and grill on rack over hot coals for 10-15 minutes, turning frequently until potato coils are crisp. Briefly lay skewers on paper towels to drain before serving.

Serves 4-6.

Note: The recipe may be doubled, but it will then be better to soak potato slices in separate bowls of hot, salted water.

PEANUT TOMATOES

4 beef tomatoes
salt and pepper
few drops Worcestershire sauce
2 teaspoons chopped fresh basil
2 teaspoons chopped fresh parsley
4 teaspoons grated Parmesan cheese
⅓ cup roasted unsalted peanuts, finely ground
knob of butter
8 bracelets of fried bread (see Note)
basil or parsley sprigs, to garnish

Rinse and dry tomatoes and halve crosswise. Season the cut surfaces of tomatoes with salt and pepper.

Sprinkle with a few drops of Worcestershire sauce. Top with basil and parsley mixed together, then sprinkle with grated Parmesan cheese. Cover with ground peanuts and add a small knob of butter to each one. Loosely wrap tomato halves separately in single thickness foil. Place cut-sides up on a rack and barbecue over hot coals for 20-25 minutes until tomatoes are soft.

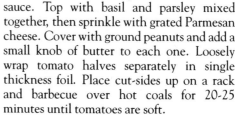
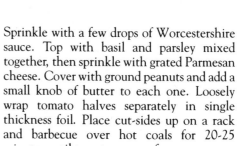
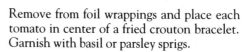

Remove from foil wrappings and place each tomato in center of a fried crouton bracelet. Garnish with basil or parsley sprigs.

Serves 4-8.

Note: The bracelets can be prepared ahead of time and will store in the freezer. Re-crisp on barbecue at the last minute. To make the bracelets, cut out 8 circles of bread from a sliced loaf and use a slightly smaller cutter to remove centers. Fry in shallow oil. Drain thoroughly.

CRUSTY GARLIC POTATOES

1 pound new potatoes
8-10 large cloves garlic
2 eggs, beaten
6-8 tablespoons yellow cornmeal
parsley sprigs, to garnish

Scrub potatoes well. Peel garlic, leaving the cloves whole.

Boil potatoes and garlic in salted water for 12-15 minutes until just cooked. Drain, reserving garlic. Skin potatoes as soon as they are cool enough to handle. Roughly chop garlic and, using a small skewer, insert pieces deeply into potatoes.

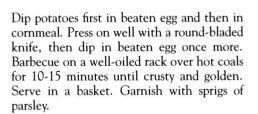

Dip potatoes first in beaten egg and then in cornmeal. Press on well with a round-bladed knife, then dip in beaten egg once more. Barbecue on a well-oiled rack over hot coals for 10-15 minutes until crusty and golden. Serve in a basket. Garnish with sprigs of parsley.

Serves 5-6.

ROASTED CORN ON THE COB

6 ears corn, with husks
½ cup butter, melted

HERBED BUTTER PATS: ¼ cup butter
1 teaspoon lemon juice
2 tablespoons chopped fresh parsley
1 tablespoon chopped fresh chives
salt and pepper

Fold back corn husks, pull out silk from corn and re-wrap husks over corn. Soak in cold water for at least 1 hour. Drain ears and shake off surplus water.

While cobs are soaking, prepare the butter pats. Beat all ingredients together until softened and well blended. Shape into a 1-inch wide roll and wrap tightly in waxed paper, maintaining cylindrical shape. Chill in freezer until firm, then slice. Arrange in a single layer on a plate and refrigerate until needed.

Pull back corn husks and brush corn with melted butter. Re-wrap corn in husks and barbecue on a rack over medium coals for 30-40 minutes, turning frequently until the husks are well browned. Remove husks and serve corn with the butter pats.

Serves 6.

Variation: After brushing corn ears with melted butter in step 3, corn ears may also be spread with peanut butter, if desired.

CHIVE & GARLIC BREAD

1 French loaf
3 cloves garlic
¼ teaspoon salt
½ cup butter
2 tablespoons snipped fresh chives

Slice loaf diagonally and deeply at about ¾-inch intervals, but do not cut through completely.

Peel garlic, place on a piece of waxed paper, sprinkle with salt and crush with flat side of a table knife. Soften butter, blend in garlic and mix in chives. Spread garlic butter between slices, covering both sides generously.

Re-shape loaf and wrap securely in foil. Place on rack and barbecue over hot coals for 10-15 minutes, turning parcel over several times. Open foil and serve at once.

Serves 6.

BROCCOLI CRÊPE ROLLS

8 ounces broccoli
⅓ cup thick plain yogurt
pepper
2 tablespoons flour
3 tablespoons milk
4 large eggs
1 tablespoon soy sauce
butter
vegetable oil

Cook broccoli in a little boiling, salted water for 6-8 minutes. Drain well and chop finely. Mix with yogurt and season well with black pepper. Cover and set aside.

Sift flour into a mixing bowl and blend in milk. Beat eggs and soy sauce together and add gradually to flour mixture, beating well to form a smooth, thin batter. Pour into a measuring jug. Heat a small omelet pan, add a knob of butter and make six or eight 6-inch thin omelet-style crêpes, browning them on one side only. (If necessary, grease pan with a little butter after making each crêpe.) Remove crêpes carefully (they set as they cool) and spread out, cooked-sides up, on non-stick paper.

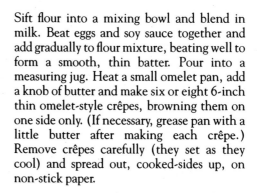

Spoon a little of the broccoli filling on one edge of the browned side of each crêpe. Fold over to enclose filling, tucking in sides and fold again to form a package. Brush cool crêpe rolls with oil and bake, starting with seam-sides down, over hot coals for 3-4 minutes on each side.

Serves 6-8.

Note: These crêpe rolls taste delicious served with a green salad.

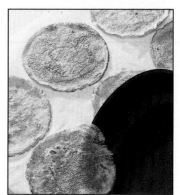

SALADS

DUCK WITH KUMQUATS

3 ounces young spinach leaves, trimmed

4 duck breast fillets, skinned

⅔ cup dry white wine

pinch ground ginger

8 coriander seeds, crushed

salt and pepper

12 kumquats, sliced

3 tablespoons hazelnut oil

2 teaspoons lemon juice

pomegranate seeds, to garnish

Wash and dry spinach and arrange on 4 plates.

Put duck breasts into a skillet and pour the wine over. Add ginger and coriander. Season with salt and pepper. Cover pan and simmer for 10 minutes until duck is tender. Add kumquats and simmer for 1 minute. Remove duck and kumquats from pan with a slotted spoon and set aside.

Simmer the liquid in the pan until reduced to ¼ cup. Stir in oil and lemon juice and heat just to warm through.

Slice the duck and arrange on the plates with the kumquats. Pour over dressing, then serve garnished with pomegranate seeds.

Serves 4 as a main course.

PEPPERY CHICKEN SALAD

2 ounces lollo rosso or radicchio

¼ head chicory

2 ounces corn salad

4 tomatoes, skinned

2 chicken breast fillets, skinned

1¼ cups dry white wine

salt and pepper

1½ teaspoons green peppercorns in brine, drained

⅓ cup light cream

Wash and dry salad leaves, tear any large ones into smaller pieces, then divide between 4 plates. Cut each tomato into 8 wedges, remove seeds, then arrange over the lettuce leaves on the plates.

Put chicken breasts into a skillet, pour wine over and season with salt and pepper. Poach for 15 minutes until chicken is tender. Lift out of pan with slotted spoon, place on a chopping board and slice.

Add the peppercorns to the cooking liquid, then boil rapidly until liquid is reduced to 5 tablespoons. Stir in cream and warm through. Arrange the chicken on the salad, pour over cream dressing and serve immediately.

Serves 4 as a main course.

HOT SAUSAGE SALAD

1 cup finely shredded red cabbage
1 cup finely shredded white cabbage
1 cooking apple
1 teaspoon lemon juice
1 pork boiling ring sausage
1 tablespoon chopped fresh parsley, to garnish
MUSTARD MAYONNAISE:
2 tablespoons mayonnaise
2 tablespoons low-fat soft cheese
2 teaspoons whole-grain mustard
2 teaspoons apple juice
salt and pepper

Put shredded cabbage into a bowl and mix together. Grate apple, toss with lemon juice, then add to cabbage.

Cook sausage according to package directions. Meanwhile, make mayonnaise by mixing ingredients together in a bowl. Stir into cabbage, then spoon onto 4 plates.

Slice cooked sausage and arrange over salad. Garnish with parsley.

Serves 4 as a main course.

THAI SEAFOOD SALAD

8 ounces monkfish, skinned and cubed
4 scallops, thawed if frozen
8 ounces salmon steak, skinned and cubed
8 raw jumbo shrimp
2-inch piece fresh ginger, shredded
2 bulbs lemon grass, peeled and chopped
scallion shreds, to garnish
MARINADE:
juice of 1 lime
4 teaspoons light soy sauce
2 teaspoons chopped fresh mint
1 tablespoon chopped fresh cilantro
1 clove garlic, crushed
WILD RICE SALAD:
3 tablespoons wild rice
1-inch piece fresh ginger, halved
3 tablespoons long-grain rice
1 tablespoon light sesame oil
6 coriander seeds, crushed

Put all seafood on to a heatproof plate, scatter ginger and lemon grass over the top.

Place an upturned saucer in a wok, add 1 cupful of water. Stand plate on saucer. Cover and steam for 5-6 minutes until the seafood is cooked. Or, use a steamer.

To make marinade, mix ingredients together in large bowl. Add cooked fish with 2 tablespoons of cooking juices. Stir gently, then leave to marinate for at least 1 hour.

To make rice salad, put wild rice and ginger into a saucepan of simmering water and cook for 30 minutes. Add long-grain rice, cook a further 20 minutes until tender.

Drain rice and discard the ginger. Stir in sesame oil and coriander seeds. Divide rice between 4 plates, arrange fish on top and spoon over marinade. Garnish with scallion shreds.

Serves 4.

SALAD NIÇOISE

4 ounces thin green beans, trimmed	
6 tomatoes, quartered	
½ cucumber, peeled and diced	
1 red pepper, seeded and sliced	
6 scallions, chopped	
7-ounce can tuna fish, drained and flaked	
1 cup pitted ripe olives	
1 tablespoon chopped fresh parsley	
3 eggs, hard-boiled	
2-ounce can anchovies, drained	
MUSTARD VINAIGRETTE DRESSING:	
¼ cup extra-virgin olive oil	
1 tablespoon red wine vinegar	
1 tablespoon lemon juice	
¼ teaspoon Dijon mustard	
salt and pepper	

Cook beans in a saucepan of water for 5-6 minutes, until just tender. Drain, rinse under cold water, then cut into 1½-inch pieces. Put into a bowl with tomatoes, cucumber, red pepper, scallions, tuna fish and olives. Mix together.

To make dressing, mix ingredients together in a bowl or screw-top jar, add to the salad with the parsley and toss gently. Quarter the hard-boiled eggs and arrange on the salad. Cut anchovy fillets in half lengthwise and arrange in criss-cross patterns on top of salad.

Serves 4.

MALAYSIAN SALAD

1¾ cups shredded white cabbage	
4 ounces thin green beans, cut into 1-inch pieces	
½ small cauliflower, divided into flowerets	
4 ounces beansprouts, trimmed	
½ cucumber	
cilantro, to garnish	
PEANUT SAUCE:	
2 tablespoons dried coconut	
⅔ cup boiling water	
3 tablespoons peanut butter	
2 teaspoons soy sauce	
juice of ½ lime	
¼ teaspoon chili powder	

To make sauce, place coconut in a bowl, pour over boiling water and leave to soak for 15 minutes.

Bring a large saucepan of water to the boil, add cabbage, beans and cauliflower and simmer for 2-3 minutes. Drain vegetables thoroughly, arrange on a platter or 4 individual plates. Scatter over beansprouts. Cut strips of skin from cucumber with a canelle knife, then slice the cucumber and arrange over salad.

Strain coconut milk into a bowl, discard the coconut, and add remaining sauce ingredients; mix well. Spoon onto center of salad or serve separately. Garnish the salad with cilantro leaves.

Serves 4.

PASTA PESTO SALAD

1⅓ cups orzo (rice-shaped pasta)

8 ounces cherry tomatoes, quartered

2 tablespoons pine nuts, lightly toasted

basil sprigs, to garnish

PESTO DRESSING:

1 ounce fresh basil leaves

2 cloves garlic, peeled

2 tablespoons pine nuts

3 tablespoons virgin olive oil

¼ cup grated Parmesan cheese

3 tablespoons light cream

Cook pasta in boiling salted water until just tender. Drain, rinse under cold water and drain again. Put into a bowl with the tomatoes.

To make the dressing, wash and dry basil leaves, then put into a blender or food processor with garlic, pine nuts and oil and work until smooth. Turn into a bowl, and beat in Parmesan cheese and cream. Stir into the pasta, then transfer to a serving dish. Serve the salad sprinkled with toasted pine nuts and garnished with a few sprigs of basil.

Serves 4.

ITALIAN SALAMI SALAD

15-ounce can haricot or cannellini beans, drained

1 bulb fennel, finely sliced

1 small green pepper, seeded and diced

4 ounces Italian salami, sliced

basil leaves, tomato wedges and ripe olives, to garnish

GARLIC DRESSING:

3 tablespoons extra-virgin olive oil

1 tablespoon white wine vinegar

1 clove garlic, crushed with salt

pepper

Put beans, fennel and green pepper into a bowl. Cut salami slices into quarters and add to the salad.

To make the dressing, mix ingredients together in a bowl or screw-top jar. Pour over the salad and toss together gently.

Spoon on to a serving dish and serve garnished with basil, tomato wedges and olives.

Serves 4.

STROGANOFF SALAD

12 ounces cold, rare cooked beef
1⅓ cups sliced button mushrooms
6 scallions, chopped or shredded
1 red pepper, seeded and sliced
shredded lettuce, to serve
SOUR CREAM DRESSING:
⅔ cup thick soured cream
1 tablespoon horseradish sauce
2 teaspoons lemon juice
salt and pepper

Cut the beef into thin strips and put into a bowl with the mushrooms, onions and pepper.

To make the dressing, mix ingredients together in a bowl. Pour over the salad and toss gently. Line a serving dish with shredded lettuce and spoon salad on top.

Serves 4.

SPANISH PAELLA SALAD

2 tablespoons olive oil
1 onion, chopped
1 clove garlic, crushed
2 cups arborio (risotto) rice
pinch saffron threads
3 cups hot chicken stock
8 ounces tomatoes, skinned, seeded and chopped
⅔-cup cooked frozen peas
2 cooked chicken breasts fillets, skinned and diced
6 ounces chorizo sausage, skinned and sliced
1 red or green pepper, seeded and sliced
stuffed olives, to garnish
PAPRIKA LEMON DRESSING:
3 tablespoons extra virgin-olive oil
1 tablespoon lemon juice
½ teaspoon paprika
salt and pepper

Put oil in a large saucepan, add onion and garlic and cook gently for 5 minutes until soft. Stir in rice and cook for 2 minutes.

Stir in the saffron threads and hot stock and simmer until rice is tender and all liquid has been absorbed. Remove from the heat, transfer to a bowl and allow to cool completely.

To make the dressing, mix all the ingredients together in a bowl or screw-top jar.

Add the skinned chopped tomatoes, peas, chicken, sausage and pepper to rice. Pour the dressing over the salad, stir gently and serve garnished with stuffed olives.

Serves 4.

EGGS TONNATO

6 large eggs, hard-boiled
1 canned pimento, cut into strips
2-ounce can anchovies, drained
dill sprigs, to garnish
TONNATO SAUCE:
1 cup mayonnaise
3½-ounce can tuna fish, drained
1 tablespoon lemon juice
1 tablespoon light cream or plain yogurt
1 teaspoon capers, drained and chopped

To make sauce, put mayonnaise into a blender or food processor with tuna fish, lemon juice and light cream or plain yogurt and work until smooth. Stir in the capers.

Halve eggs lengthwise and arrange on 4 plates. Spoon the sauce over the eggs and decorate with strips of pimento. Halve the anchovy fillets, then curl them around and place between the eggs. Serve the eggs garnished with sprigs of dill.

Serves 4.

PASTA & SHRIMP SALAD

8 ounces pasta shells
12 ounces cooked shelled shrimp
4 ounces smoked salmon, cut into strips
tarragon sprigs, to garnish
HERB DRESSING:
3 tablespoons virgin olive oil
1 tablespoon lemon juice
1 tablespoon tomato juice
1 tablespoon chopped fresh parsley
1 tablespoon chopped fresh tarragon
salt and pepper

Cook pasta in boiling salted water until just tender. Drain, rinse under cold water and drain again. Put into a bowl with shrimp and salmon.

To make the dressing, mix ingredients together in a bowl or screw-top jar. Pour over the salad, toss gently, then transfer to a serving dish. Serve garnished with sprigs of tarragon.

Serves 4.

BARBECUED STEAK SALAD

four 6-ounce boneless sirloin steaks

mixed salad leaves

cherry tomatoes, to garnish

MARINADE:

¼ cup sunflower oil

2 tablespoons red wine vinegar

1 tablespoon tomato paste

2 teaspoons Worcestershire sauce

1 teaspoon Dijon mustard

1 clove garlic, crushed

½ teaspoon paprika

salt and pepper

AVOCADO DRESSING:

1 ripe avocado

juice of 1 lemon

¼ cup virgin olive oil

1 clove garlic, crushed

¼ cup light cream

To make the marinade, put all the ingredients into a dish and mix together. Add the steaks, turn to coat then leave for 1 hour.

To make the dressing, halve the avocado, remove seed and scoop out flesh. Place in blender or food processor with remaining ingredients and work until smooth. Season with salt and pepper.

Arrange salad leaves on 4 plates. Either cook steaks on a barbecue or under a hot broiler for 6-8 minutes, turning them once. Transfer cooked steaks to a board, slice them into strips and arrange on the plates. Spoon over dressing. Serve garnished with cherry tomatoes.

Serves 4.

Note: The dressing should be used within 2 hours of being made.

HERRINGSALAT

4 fresh herrings, cleaned, scaled and backbone removed

2 pickled gherkins, diced

1⅓ cups diced cooked potatoes

½ bunch scallions, chopped

8 ounces cooked beet, sliced

chives, to garnish

CIDER MARINADE:

½ cup cider vinegar

½ cup water

2 tablespoons sugar

1 small onion, chopped

1 bay leaf

good pinch pepper

good pinch ground allspice

YOGURT MAYONNAISE DRESSING:

6 tablespoons plain yogurt

2 tablespoons mayonnaise

Cut herring fillets into 2-inch pieces and put into a glass dish.

To prepare the marinade, combine ingredients in a saucepan and bring to a boil. Simmer for 1 minute, then leave to cool. Pour over herrings, and marinate overnight or for at least 6 hours.

Drain herrings from marinade and put into a bowl with gherkins, potatoes and scallions. To make the dressing, mix ingredients together, then stir into salad.

Arrange sliced beet around edge of serving dish, spoon salad in center and garnish with chives.

Serves 4.

SMOKED MACKEREL SALAD

1 pound new potatoes
1 tablespoon olive oil
4 smoked mackerel fillets
½ cucumber, peeled
parsley sprigs, to garnish
MUSTARD DRESSING:
2 tablespoons sunflower oil
1 tablespoon whole-grain mustard
1 tablespoon lemon juice

In a saucepan of boiling water, cook potatoes in their skins until tender; drain. When cool enough to handle, remove skins, slice potatoes thickly, or quarter. Put into a bowl and toss with olive oil.

Remove skin from mackerel and discard. Break fish into pieces and add to potatoes. Cut cucumber in half crosswise; dice one half and add to salad.

To make the dressing, mix ingredients together in a bowl or screw-top jar. Stir into the salad, then spoon on to a serving dish. Using an apple corer, remove center from remaining piece of cucumber and discard. Slice cucumber. Serve the salad garnished with cucumber slices and parsley.

Serves 4.

DRESSED CRAB

1 pound cooked crab
1 teaspoon lemon juice
1 tablespoon mayonnaise
½ cup fresh bread crumbs
salt and pepper
1 egg, hard-boiled
1 tablespoon chopped fresh parsley
lettuce leaves and lemon slices, to garnish

Hold crab firmly, twist off two claws and legs. Pull body section from shell, discarding feathery gills, the grayish-white stomach sac behind the head and any green matter.

Using a teaspoon, scrape into a bowl all brown meat inside shell. Discard inner membrane attached on either side. Press natural dark line on underside of shell to break along the line neatly; discard the broken inner shell. Wash and dry the main shell.

Snap legs in half by bending backward at joint. Using a hammer, gently crack all shells; scrape white meat into a second bowl, using a skewer to get into crevices. Discard any bits of shell. Crack large claws, remove meat and add to bowl. Cut body section in half, pick out white meat from honeycomb structure and add to bowl.

To dress the crab, mix brown meat with lemon juice, mayonnaise and bread crumbs and season with salt and pepper. Flake white meat with fork. Spoon brown mixture in a line in center of shell. Carefully place white meat on either side.

Separate hard-boiled egg; sieve yolk and chop white. Cover dark meat with egg yolk, sprinkle a line of egg white on either side of this, then a line of parsley. Garnish with lemon slices and lettuce and serve with extra mayonnaise.

Serves 1.

CHEF'S SALAD

½ iceberg lettuce
½ Boston lettuce
4 sticks celery, sliced
½ bunch radishes, sliced
6 ounces cold cooked chicken
4 ounces sliced ham
4 ounces Emmental cheese
BLUE CHEESE DRESSING:
3 tablespoons plain yogurt
3 tablespoons mayonnaise
⅓ cup rinded and crumbled Danish blue
or Roquefort cheese
1 teaspoon lemon juice

Shred iceberg lettuce, tear the Boston into smaller pieces and put into a salad bowl with the celery and radishes. Cut the chicken, ham and cheese into strips and add to the salad.

To make the dressing, put ingredients into a blender or food processor and work until smooth. Pour over salad and toss gently to coat all the leaves.

Serves 4.

MARINATED BEEF SALAD

1 pound sirloin steak
½ head bok choy
1 large carrot
2 scallions, thinly sliced
1 tomato, to garnish
TERIYAKI MARINADE:
6 tablespoons dry sherry
3 tablespoons soy sauce
1 tablespoon red wine vinegar
2 tablespoons clear honey
1 clove garlic, crushed
1 teaspoon ground ginger

To make the marinade, put all the ingredients into a bowl and mix together. Add beef, turn to coat with marinade. Cover and leave to marinate in the refrigerator overnight, turning meat once.

Preheat oven to 425F. Drain the meat, put into a baking dish, and cook in the oven for 25 minutes.

Remove from oven, pour the juices into a measuring jug, and leave to cool.

Arrange bok choy leaves on a platter. Place cooled meat, cut-side down on a board, slice downward to give oval-shaped slices, then arrange these on the leaves. Skim fat from reserved cooking juices and discard. Drizzle juices over meat.

Using a potato peeler, cut thin ribbons from outside of carrot, discarding center. Cut these ribbons into fine strips. Scatter the strips around the edge of the dish.

Scatter scallions over the meat. With a sharp knife, cut peel from tomato and gently roll up to make a rose to garnish the center of the salad.

Serves 4.

SAFFRON RICE RING

2 tablespoons butter

4 cardamom pods

3 cloves

2-inch piece cinnamon stick

1¼ cups basmati rice

2 cups hot chicken stock

good pinch saffron threads

⅔ cup frozen petit pois

salt and pepper

3 tablespoons light cream

mint sprigs and shelled shrimp,

to garnish

FILLING:

8 ounces shelled cooked shrimps

½ cucumber, diced

¼ cup plain yogurt

2 teaspoons chopped fresh mint

pinch cayenne pepper

In a large saucepan, melt butter, add cardamoms, cloves and cinnamon stick and fry for 1 minute. Stir in rice and cook for 1 minute.

Gradually stir in hot chicken stock, keeping it simmering as it is added. Simmer rice for 15 minutes.

Meanwhile, put saffron into a cup, pour on 2 tablespoons hot water. Stir into rice with peas and continue to cook for 2 minutes. Remove from the heat and season to taste with salt and pepper.

Remove cardamoms, cloves and cinnamon stick, then stir in cream. Spoon rice into a 5-cup ring mold, pressing down with the back of spoon. Cool, then refrigerate for 30 minutes.

Invert rice ring onto a plate. To make filling, mix all the ingredients together in a bowl, then spoon into center of rice ring. Serve garnished with sprigs of mint and shrimp.

*Serves 4 as a main course or
6 as a side salad.*

TONNO CON FAGIOLI

15-ounce can cannellini or borlotti beans, drained

14-ounce can flageolets (green kidney beans), drained

½ red onion, sliced

salt and pepper

two 7-ounce cans tuna fish, drained

2 tablespoons chopped fresh parsley

ripe olives, lemon slices and parsley, to garnish

DRESSING:

⅓ cup virgin olive oil

1 tablespoon red wine vinegar

Put beans and flageolets into a bowl with onion and season with salt and pepper. Add tuna fish, breaking it into large flakes. Stir in parsley.

To make the dressing, put ingredients in a bowl or screw-top jar, mix well, then add to salad. Toss gently, then transfer to dish. Serve garnished with ripe olives, lemon slices and parsley.

*Serves 4 as a main course and
6 as a starter.*

MEDITERRANEAN LENTILS

1¼ cups brown or green lentils
1⅓ cups skinned, seeded and diced tomatoes
3 sticks celery, sliced
⅔ cup sliced button mushrooms
celery leaves and lemon slices, to garnish
SPICY LEMON DRESSING:
⅓ cup virgin olive oil
1 tablespoon lemon juice
1 clove garlic, crushed
1 tablespoon chopped fresh parsley
½ teaspoon ground cumin
salt and pepper

Put the lentils in a strainer and rinse thoroughly, then tip into a saucepan and cover with water. Bring to a boil, then simmer for 30 minutes until tender. Drain and put into a bowl with the tomatoes, celery and mushrooms.

To make the dressing. Put all the ingredients in a bowl or screw-top jar and mix well. Pour over the salad and stir. Serve garnished with celery leaves and lemon slices.

Serves 6 as a side salad.

BULGAR MEDLEY

2 tablespoons sunflower oil
2 shallots, chopped
1 clove garlic, crushed
2 cups bulgar wheat
2 cups hot vegetable stock
2 carrots, diced
3 sticks celery, sliced
3 leeks, sliced
2 zucchini, diced
fresh mint leaves, to garnish
GARLIC TOMATO DRESSING:
1⅓ cups skinned, seeded and finely chopped tomatoes
3 tablespoons virgin olive oil
1 tablespoon wine vinegar
1 teaspoon tomato paste
1 clove garlic, crushed
½ teaspoon paprika
pinch sugar
salt and pepper

Heat oil in a saucepan, add shallots and garlic and cook for 2-3 minutes. Add bulgar wheat and stir for 1 minute over a medium heat. Gradually pour in hot stock and simmer for 5 minutes. Add carrots, celery and leeks and cook for 5 minutes. Stir in zucchini and cook for a further 2 minutes. Set aside.

To make the dressing, mix all the ingredients together in a bowl, then stir into bulgar salad. Leave to cool, then check the seasoning. Serve garnished with fresh mint leaves.

Serves 6-8 as a side salad.

Variation: Other lightly cooked vegetables can be substituted for the ones used here.

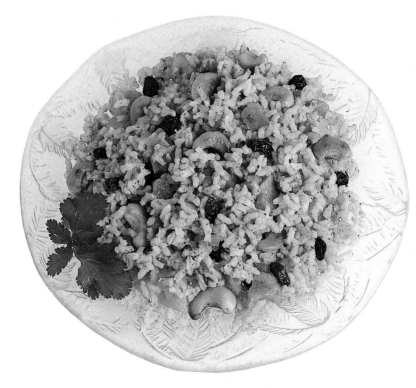

BUTTER BEAN SALAD

1⅓ cups dried butter beans, soaked
overnight

salt

6 slices bacon

snipped chives, to garnish

TOMATO DRESSING:

1 cup skinned, seeded and chopped
tomatoes

1 teaspoon tomato paste

3 tablespoons extra-virgin olive oil

2 teaspoons lemon juice

salt and pepper

Rinse butter beans, put into a
saucepan, cover with water and
simmer for about 1 hour until

tender. Add salt during last 5
minutes of cooking.

Meanwhile, cook bacon in a
skillet until crisp. Remove from the
pan and drain on paper towels, then
crumble into small pieces.

To make the dressing, put all the
ingredients into a blender and work
until tomatoes are pulpy. Drain
beans, put into a serving dish and
pour the dressing over. Mix in the
crumbled bacon. Leave to cool.
Serve garnished with snipped
chives.

Serves 4-6 as a side salad.

CURRIED RICE SALAD

½ cup chopped semi-dried apricots

1⅓ cups long-grain brown rice

3 tablespoons sunflower oil

⅓ cup cashew nuts

1 onion, chopped

1 teaspoon cumin seeds

1 tablespoon curry powder

⅓ cup orange juice

⅓ cup raisins

salt and pepper

cilantro sprigs, to garnish

Put chopped apricots in a bowl,
pour over sufficient boiling water to
cover and leave to soak for 45
minutes.

Meanwhile, cook rice in boiling
salted water for 40 minutes until
tender.

Heat the oil in a skillet, add
cashew nuts and fry until golden.

Remove with a slotted spoon and
drain on paper towels. Add onion
to pan and cook over a medium
heat for 3-4 minutes. Stir in cumin
seeds and curry powder and cook for
2 minutes. Pour in orange juice
and simmer for 1 minute. Remove
from heat.

Drain rice, rinse under cold run-
ning water, then drain again. Put
into a large bowl, add the warm
curry sauce and mix well.

Drain apricots and stir into rice
with nuts and raisins. Season with
salt and pepper. Allow the salad to
stand for at least 2 hours before
serving to allow flavors to mingle.
Serve garnished with sprigs of fresh
cilantro.

Serves 6 as a side salad.

MEXICAN BEAN SALAD

14-ounce can red kidney beans, drained
1 cup cooked corn kernels
1 green pepper, seeded and chopped
½ bunch scallions, chopped
2 tablespoons chopped fresh cilantro
½ iceberg lettuce, shredded, if desired
lime slices and flat-leaved parsley sprigs, to garnish
LIME DRESSING:
¼ cup virgin olive oil
juice of ½ lime
1 clove garlic, crushed
salt and pepper

Put the kidney beans, corn, green pepper, scallions and cillantro into a bowl.

To make the dressing, put all the ingredients into a bowl or screw-top jar and mix well. Pour over the salad and toss together.

Line a serving dish with the shredded iceberg lettuce, if desired, and spoon the bean mixture on top. Serve the salad garnished with lime slices and sprigs of parsley.

Serves 4-6 as a side salad.

TABBOULEH

1⅓ cups bulgar wheat
¼ cup lemon juice
¼ cup virgin olive oil
1 tablespoon finely chopped Spanish onion
6 scallions, finely chopped
large bunch flat-leaved parsley, chopped
½ cup fresh mint, chopped
salt and pepper
1 Cos lettuce
cherry tomatoes and parsley sprigs, to garnish

Put bulgar into a bowl, cover with warm water and leave to soak for 30 minutes. Squeeze out excess water and put bulgar into a bowl. Add lemon juice, oil, onion, scallions, parsley and mint and season to taste with salt and pepper. Mix together, then chill for at least 1 hour for flavors to blend.

To serve, arrange Cos lettuce leaves around the edge of a platter, spoon salad in the center and garnish with cherry tomatoes and sprigs of parsley.

Serves 6.

SPICED CHICK-PEA SALAD

2 cups dried chick-peas, soaked overnight
2 tablespoons chopped fresh cilantro and
cilantro sprigs, to garnish
CILANTRO DRESSING:
3 tablespoons olive oil
1 small onion, chopped
1 green chili, seeded and finely chopped
1 clove garlic, finely chopped
2 teaspoons ground coriander
1 teaspoon ground cumin
1 teaspoon turmeric
salt and pepper
2 tablespoons plain yogurt

Drain chick-peas from soaking water and put into a saucepan with fresh water. Bring to a boil, and simmer for 1 hour or until tender.

Meanwhile, make the dressing. Heat oil in a small skillet, add onion, chili and garlic and cook for 2-3 minutes. Stir in spices and cook for 1 minute. Season to taste with salt and pepper. Turn into a large bowl and stir in the yogurt.

Drain chick-peas, cool briefly then remove skins while still warm. Add to spice mixture and mix well. Leave to marinate for at least 2 hours. Serve garnished.

Serves 6 as a side salad.

JAPANESE VINEGARED SALAD

4 ounces snow peas, trimmed
1 cup long-grain rice
JAPANESE DRESSING:
2 tablespoons rice vinegar
1 tablespoon light sesame oil
1 teaspoon dark sesame oil
4 teaspoons tamari (Japanese soy sauce)
4 scallions, chopped

Blanch the snow peas in a saucepan of boiling water for 30 seconds, drain, rinse under cold water, then dry on paper towels. Arrange around edge of serving dish.

Cook rice in boiling salted water for 10-12 minutes until tender. Drain, rinse with cold water, then drain again. Put rice into a bowl. To make the dressing, mix ingredients together in a bowl or screw-top jar. Stir into rice. Spoon rice into serving dish and serve.

Serves 4-6.

Variation: The dressed rice can be wrapped in small blanched spinach or grape leaves. Cut the packages in half, then stand them on end to resemble Japanese sushi.

HUMMUS SALAD

15-ounce can chick-peas, drained
¼ cup virgin olive oil
3 tablespoons tahini (sesame seed paste)
2 cloves garlic
juice of 1 lemon
salt and pepper
1 teaspoon paprika
olives and cilantro leaves, to garnish
TO SERVE:
carrot sticks or baby carrots
celery sticks
radishes

Put chick-peas in a blender or food processor with 3 tablespoons of oil, tahini, garlic and lemon juice. Work until smooth, then season.

Spoon into a serving bowl or 4 individual dishes. Drizzle remaining oil over and dust with paprika.

Garnish and serve with the raw fresh vegetables.

Serves 4 as a appetizer or light meal.

THREE BEAN SALAD

⅔ cup dried red kidney beans, soaked overnight
salt and pepper
1 cup trimmed and sliced thin green beans
8 ounces shelled lima beans
shallot rings, to garnish
SHALLOT DRESSING:
¼ cup virgin olive oil
1 tablespoon red wine vinegar
1 shallot, finely chopped

Put red kidney beans into a saucepan with water to cover and boil for 1½ hours until tender, adding salt 5 minutes before the end of the cooking time. Drain, put into a bowl, and leave to cool.

Cook green beans and lima beans in boiling salted water for about 5 minutes until just tender. Drain, skin lima beans, and add both beans to the kidney beans.

To make the dressing, mix ingredients together in a bowl or screwtop jar, seasoning to taste with salt and pepper. Pour over the salad and toss. Transfer to a serving dish, cover and refrigerate until required. Serve garnished with shallot rings.

Serves 4-6.

THOUSAND ISLAND SALAD

1½ pounds firm white fish, such as bass, cod, halibut, swordfish, monkfish

juice of 1 lemon

salt and pepper

2 kiwi fruit

2 tamarillos

1 small mango

paprika and parsley sprigs, to garnish

THOUSAND ISLAND DRESSING:

1 cup mayonnaise

1 teaspoon tomato paste

3 teaspoons lemon juice

6 stuffed green olives, chopped

2 scallions, finely chopped

1 tablespoon chopped fresh parsley

1 hard-boiled egg, chopped

½ teaspoon paprika

½ teaspoon sugar

Preheat oven to 375F. Skin the fish and put into a baking dish, sprinkle over lemon juice and season with salt and pepper. Cook in the oven for 15-20 minutes. Allow to cool, then cut into cubes. Spoon over a little of the cooking juices to keep the fish moist.

Meanwhile, make the dressing by mixing all the ingredients together in a bowl.

Prepare the fruit. Peel the kiwi fruit and tamarillos, then slice. Peel the mango and cut into strips.

Divide the fish between 4 plates, arrange the tropical fruits around the fish, then either spoon over the dressing or serve it on one side. Garnish fish with a little paprika and sprigs of parsley.

Serves 4 as a main course.

GINGER PORK & LYCHEES

2 tablespoons light sesame oil

1 pound pork tenderloin, cut into strips

1 clove garlic, crushed

1 tablespoon chopped fresh ginger

3 ounces snow peas, cut into thin strips

15-ounce can lychees, drained

½ head bok choy leaves

chili flowers, to garnish

SWEET AND SOUR DRESSING:

2 tablespoons light sesame oil

4 teaspoons rice vinegar

2 teaspoons dark soy sauce

1 teaspoon honey

1 teaspoon tomato paste

Heat oil in a large skillet or wok, add pork, garlic and ginger and cook until pork is browned. Add snow peas and cook for 30 seconds. Remove from heat, transfer with a slotted spoon, and add lychees.

To make the dressing, mix ingredients together in a bowl. Pour over salad, then leave to cool.

Shred bok choy leaves, arrange on serving platter or dishes. Spoon salad on top, garnish and serve.

Serves 4 as a main course.

CHICKEN & GRAPE SALAD

3 cups cooked cold chicken
3 sticks celery, chopped
4 ounces black grapes
4 ounces green grapes
½ lettuce, finely shredded, if desired
nasturtium flowers and tarragon sprigs, to garnish
TARRAGON CREAM DRESSING:
3 tablespoons virgin olive oil
1 tablespoon tarragon vinegar
3 tablespoons thick soured cream
salt and pepper

Put chicken and celery in a bowl. Halve grapes, remove seeds and add to the bowl.

To make the dressing, mix all the ingredients together in a bowl or screw-top jar. Pour over salad and toss together. Divide lettuce, if using, between 4 plates and spoon chicken salad on top. Garnish with nasturtium flowers and tarragon.

Serves 4 as a main course.

ROLLMOP & APPLE SALAD

8 rollmop herrings
2 green eating apples
2 tablespoons lemon juice
1 bulb fennel, finely sliced
hard-boiled egg slices and dill sprigs, to garnish
SOUR CREAM DILL DRESSING:
⅔ cup thick soured cream
2 tablespoons plain yogurt
2 teaspoons creamed horseradish sauce
1 tablespoon chopped fresh dill
salt and pepper

Cut rollmops into bite-sized pieces and put into a bowl. Core and chop apples, put into a second bowl with lemon juice; toss to prevent discoloration. Remove apple and add to the herrings with the fennel.

To make the dressing, mix ingredients together in a bowl, then stir into the salad. Serve garnished with hard-boiled egg and dill.

Serves 4 as a main course.

CHEESE & FRUIT PLATTER

| 2 green eating apples |
| juice of ½ lemon |
| 4 ounces smoked cheese, cubed |
| 8 ounces brie, or 1 whole camembert, sliced |
| 4 sticks celery, sliced |
| 6 ounces grapes |
| celery leaves, to garnish |
| LEMON MAYONNAISE: |
| ½ cup mayonnaise |
| ½ teaspoon finely grated lemon peel |
| 2 teaspoons lemon juice |

Quarter and core the apples, then slice and place in a bowl with the lemon juice. Stir to coat. Arrange cubed and sliced cheese and the apple slices on 4 plates.

Add the celery and grapes. Garnish with celery leaves. To make the mayonnaise, mix all the ingredients together in a bowl. Serve the mayonnaise separately.

Serves 4.

TURKEY & CRANBERRY SALAD

| 1 pound turkey escalopes |
| 2 tablespoons virgin olive oil |
| 1 small onion, chopped |
| ⅔ cup fresh or frozen cranberries |
| grated peel of ½ orange |
| orange slices and watercress sprigs, to garnish |
| MARINADE: |
| juice of 1 lime |
| ½ cup dry vermouth |
| 2 teaspoons clear honey |
| ½ teaspoon dry oregano |
| salt and pepper |

Cut the turkey escalopes into thin strips. Mix marinade ingredients together in a bowl. Add turkey strips and marinate for 2 hours.

Remove turkey from marinade with a slotted spoon; reserve marinade. Heat oil in a fskillet, add turkey and onion and sauté for 5 minutes. Pour reserved marinade into the pan with the cranberries and orange peel and cook gently until the cranberries begin to split. Transfer the mixture to a dish to cool.

Stir the salad and spoon into a serving dish. Serve garnished with orange slices and sprigs of watercress.

Serves 3-4 as a main course.

ENDIVE & ORANGE SALAD

⅓ cup hazelnuts

4 heads endive, chopped

3 oranges

1 tablespoon chopped fresh parsley

HAZELNUT DRESSING:

3 tablespoons hazelnut oil

3 tablespoons orange juice

pinch apple pie spice

salt and pepper

Place hazelnuts on cookie sheet and brown under a hot broiler until the skins begin to crack. Allow to cool a little, then rub off the skins. Roughly chop the nuts. Put endive in a large bowl.

Cut peel and pith from oranges. Holding each one over a bowl to catch juice, cut into segments. Cut the segments in half and add to the endive.

To make the dressing, add all the ingredients to the juice in a bowl, mix well, then pour over the salad. Toss gently, then transfer to a serving dish. Scatter over the hazelnuts and serve garnished with chopped parsley.

Serves 4-6 as a side salad.

AVOCADO & CITRUS SALAD

½ chicory, torn into pieces

2 oranges

1 grapefruit

1 ripe avocado

CITRUS DRESSING:

1 tablespoon sunflower oil

peel and juice of ½ lime

1 tablespoon chopped fresh mint

salt and pepper

Put chicory into a salad bowl. Cut peel and pith from oranges and grapefruit. Holding each one over a bowl to catch juice, remove segments and halve. Arrange on top of chicory.

Halve avocado, remove seed, slice or dice flesh, then add to salad.

To make the dressing, mix all the ingredients in a bowl or screw-top jar with 2 tablespoons of juice. Spoon over salad, and serve.

Serves 4 as a side salad.

PERSIAN CARROT SALAD

2¾ cups grated carrots
2 large oranges
½ cup raisins
⅓ cup blanched almonds, lightly toasted
lime slices, to garnish
SPICY DRESSING:
2 tablespoons virgin olive oil
2 tablespoons lime juice
1 teaspoon ground cumin
½ teaspoon ground cinnamon
½ teaspoon sugar

Put carrots into a bowl. Cut peel
and pith from oranges. Remove segments and chop. Add to carrots with
raisins and almonds.

To make the dressing, mix all the
ingredients together in a bowl or
screw-top jar. Add to salad. Toss
together, then refrigerate for 1 hour.
Serve garnished with lime slices.

Serves 6 as a side salad.

ASPARAGUS & AVOCADO SALAD

1 pound asparagus spears
1 ripe avocado
4 teaspoons chopped pistachio nuts or walnuts
fennel sprigs and orange segments, to garnish
MARINADE:
½ cup walnut oil
2 tablespoons orange juice
2 teaspoons grated orange peel
2 teaspoons light soft brown sugar
½ teaspoon salt
½ teaspoon black pepper
2 teaspoons Dijon mustard
6 teaspoons chopped fresh fennel

Trim asparagus spears and, using a
sharp knife, peel outside skin off
each stem. Cook asparagus in large
shallow saucepan of boiling salted
water for 5-8 minutes, until tender.
Drain and cool.

To make marinade, mix oil,
orange juice, peel, sugar, salt,
pepper, mustard and fennel
together, stirring until well
blended.

Place asparagus spears in a
shallow dish, pour over marinade
and turn each spear in marinade to
coat evenly. Cover with plastic
wrap and leave in a cool place for 1
hour or until ready to serve.

Lift out asparagus and arrange on
4 individual serving plates. Peel
and dice avocado and add to marinade with pistachios or walnuts,
turning gently.

Spoon avocado and nut mixture
over centers of asparagus spears and
garnish with sprigs of fennel and
orange segments.

Serves 4.

FRUITY COLESLAW

2 cups finely shredded white or light green cabbage
14-ounce can pineapple slices or 2 cups chopped fresh pineapple
1½ eating apples
2 teaspoons lemon juice
½ cup raisins
⅓ cup salted peanuts
½ apple, sliced, to garnish
DRESSING:
1 cup mayonnaise
1 teaspoon clear honey
3 tablespoons pineapple or apple juice
salt
black pepper

Put cabbage into a large bowl. If using canned pineapple, drain well, reserving the juice, and chop the fruit. Add pineapple to cabbage.

Core and chop apples, toss in lemon juice and add to salad with raisins and peanuts.

To make the dressing, mix all the ingredients in a bowl, using reserved pineapple juice or apple juice, then pour over the salad. Mix well, then turn into a serving dish. Garnish and serve at once.

Serves 6-8 as a side salad.

APPLE & CELERY ROOT SALAD

1 celery root
3 eating apples
2 tablespoons lemon juice
POPPY SEED DRESSING:
2 tablespoons poppy seeds
¼ cup thick plain yogurt
3 tablespoons apple juice
salt and pepper

Peel celery root; cut into ½-inch thick slices. Put into a saucepan of boiling water and simmer for 7-8 minutes until just tender. Drain and leave to cool.

Cut apples into quarters; remove cores. Slice 4 quarters; dice remainder. Put all the apple into a bowl with lemon juice and toss together.

Remove apple slices, put to one side for garnishing. Dice the celery root and mix with the diced apples.

To make the dressing, mix all the ingredients together in a screw-top jar, then pour over the salad and toss together. Transfer to a serving dish and serve garnished with apple slices.

Serves 6 as a side salad.

CLASSIC TOMATO SALAD

1 pound firm tomatoes
1 teaspoon sugar
salt and pepper
⅓ cup virgin olive oil
2 tablespoons white wine vinegar
1 tablespoon snipped fresh chives
chopped mixed fresh herbs, to garnish

Slice tomatoes thinly and arrange on a serving plate. Sprinkle with sugar and season with salt and pepper. Mix oil and vinegar together in a bowl or screw-top jar, then spoon over the salad.

Scatter over chives, then cover salad and refrigerate for a least 1 hour before serving. Garnish with mixed herbs.

Serves 4-6.

Variation: Sprinkle tomatoes with finely chopped scallion or shredded basil instead of chives.

GERMAN POTATO SALAD

2 pounds potatoes, scrubbed
6 scallions, finely chopped
salt and pepper
3 tablespoons mayonnaise
3 tablespoons plain yogurt
snipped chives, to garnish

Cook unpeeled potatoes in a saucepan of boiling salted water for about 15 minutes until tender.

Drain, then cool a little before removing skins. Cool completely. Dice potatoes and put into a bowl with scallions, then season with salt and pepper.

Mix mayonnaise and yogurt together in a bowl, then fold into the salad. Spoon into serving dish and serve garnished with chives.

Serves 6.

Note: The potato skins can be left on if preferred.

COLESLAW

2⅔ cups shredded white cabbage

2 carrots, coarsely grated

5 sticks celery, sliced

2 tablespoons chopped fresh parsley

celery leaves, to garnish

BOILED DRESSING:

2 tablespoons sunflower oil

1 tablespoon flour

2 teaspoons vinegar

1 teaspoon dry mustard

1 egg, beaten

salt and pepper

pinch cayenne pepper

Put cabbage, carrots, celery and parsley into a bowl and mix well.

To make the dressing, blend oil and flour in a saucepan, add ½ cup water, the vinegar, mustard, egg and seasonings. Cook over a very low heat until thickened, stirring all the time. Cool slightly, then pour over the salad and mix well. Cool before serving garnished with celery leaves.

Serves 6-8.

GREEK SALAD

½ Cos lettuce, chopped

a few young spinach leaves, shredded

3 tomatoes, cut into wedges

½ cucumber, halved lengthwise and sliced

½ Spanish onion, cut into rings

1 green pepper, seeded and sliced

6 ounces feta cheese, cubed

12 ripe olives

1 teaspoon chopped fresh oregano

LEMON DRESSING:

¼ cup extra-virgin olive oil

1 tablespoon lemon juice

salt and pepper

Put lettuce, spinach, tomatoes, cucumber, onion and pepper into a bowl. Top with cheese and olives; sprinkle with oregano.

Mix dressing ingredients. Spoon over the salad and serve.

Serves 4.

CAULIFLOWER SALAD

| 1 cauliflower |
| 1 bunch radishes, trimmed and sliced |
| toasted sesame seeds |
| radishes, to garnish |
| TAHINI DRESSING: |
| ⅔ cup plain yogurt |
| 4 teaspoons tahini (sesame seed paste) |
| 1 teaspoon clear honey |

Break cauliflower into small flowerets, blanch in a saucepan of boiling water for 2 minutes, drain and cool. Put into a bowl with radishes.

To make the dressing, mix all the ingredients together in a bowl. Pour onto salad and mix well. Spoon into a serving dish and sprinkle with sesame seeds. Serve garnished with radishes.

Serves 6.

FRENCH POTATO SALAD

| 1½ pounds new potatoes, scrubbed |
| 1 tablespoon virgin olive oil |
| 2 tablespoons chopped mixed herbs and herb sprigs |
| HERB VINAIGRETTE: |
| 3 tablespoons virgin olive oil |
| 1 tablespoon white wine vinegar |
| salt and pepper |

Boil unpeeled potatoes in a saucepan of salted water for about 15 minutes until tender. Drain. If they are small leave whole, otherwise cool a little, then cut into slices, halves or quarters. Put into a bowl and, while still warm, pour over 1 tablespoon oil. Leave to cool.

To make the dressing, mix together oil and vinegar in a bowl or screw-top jar. Season with salt and pepper, then stir into potatoes. Just before serving, sprinkle with chopped herbs and gently fold in. Garnish with sprigs of herbs.

Serves 4-6.

ZUCCHINI SALAD

| 2 cups coarsely grated zucchini |
| salt |
| fresh herbs or baby zucchini and flowers, to garnish |
| HERB YOGURT MAYONNAISE: |
| 2 tablespoons mayonnaise |
| 2 teaspoons chopped fresh parsley |
| 2 teaspoons chopped fresh tarragon |
| 2 teaspoons chopped fresh chervil |
| 2 teaspoons chopped fresh chives |
| ¼ cup plain yogurt |
| pepper |

Place zucchini on 3 layers of paper towels, sprinkle with salt and leave for 1 hour.

To make the dressing, mix all the ingredients together in a large bowl. Add zucchini to dressing and stir together.

Spoon into a serving dish and serve garnished with fresh herbs or baby zucchini and flowers.

Serves 6.

TRICOLOR PASTA SALAD

| 8 ounces tricolored pasta twists |
| salt |
| 1 tablespoon virgin olive oil |
| 1 cup sliced open-caped mushrooms, (use wild mushrooms if available) |
| ½ cup pitted and chopped green olives |
| 2-ounce can anchovies, drained and cut into thin strips |
| 1 tablespoon chopped fresh oregano |
| oregano sprigs, to garnish |
| DRESSING: |
| 2 tablespoons virgin olive oil |
| 1 tablespoon balsamico vinegar |
| pepper |

Cook pasta in boiling salted water for 5-6 minutes until just tender, then drain and rinse.

Heat the oil in a skillet and cook mushrooms for 2-3 minutes. Cool, then put into a bowl with cooked pasta, olives, anchovies and oregano.

To make the dressing, mix together the oil and vinegar and season with pepper. Pour over the salad and toss together. Serve garnished with sprigs of oregano.

Serves 4–6.

SWEET PEPPER SALAD

2 large red peppers
2 large yellow peppers
⅓ cup extra-virgin olive oil
2 cloves garlic
salt and pepper
ripe olives and fresh parsley, to garnish

Put peppers under a hot broiler, turning them until skins are blistered and black all over. Place in a plastic bag and leave to cool for 10-15 minutes. Peel skins off, remove stems and seeds and cut flesh into strips. Arrange in a shallow dish.

Drizzle olive oil over peppers. Peel garlic, cut into slivers and scatter over peppers. Season with salt and pepper, then leave to marinate for 24 hours.

Serve garnished with ripe olives and parsley.

Serves 4-6.

SUMMER RATATOUILLE

¼ cup virgin olive oil
1 bulb fennel, sliced
1 large onion, sliced
1 clove garlic, crushed
1 large tomato, peeled and chopped
1 red pepper, seeded
1 yellow pepper, seeded
1 green pepper, seeded
3 cups sliced zucchini
1 teaspoon chopped fresh thyme
salt and pepper
shredded basil leaves and fennel fronds, to garnish

Heat oil in a large saucepan, add fennel, onion and garlic, cover and cook gently for 5 minutes. Add tomato; cook for 10 minutes.

Cut peppers into dice, add to pan with zucchini and thyme. Season with salt and pepper and cook for a further 5 minutes. Leave to cool.

Spoon the salad into a serving dish and serve garnished with basil leaves and fennel fronds.

Serves 6.

MOROCCAN SUGARED LETTUCE

1 crisp, curly-leaf lettuce
4 ounces fresh dates, halved and pitted
3 satsumas or clementines
2 tablespoons sugar
3 tablespoons white wine vinegar
pepper

Shred lettuce, then put into salad bowl with the dates.

With a zester, peel shreds of peel from one satsuma or clementine; reserve. Remove peel and pith from fruit, then cut fruit into slices. Break slices into smaller pieces and add to bowl. Sprinkle sugar over and toss salad, then sprinkle over vinegar and toss again. Season with pepper and serve garnished with reserved shreds of peel.

Serves 6.

RADISH SALAD

1 mouli (white radish), weighing about 8 ounces
salt
1 bunch radishes, trimmed and quartered
1 tablespoon sesame seeds
radish leaves, to garnish
SESAME VINAIGRETTE:
1 tablespoon sunflower oil
1 teaspoon dark sesame oil
2 teaspoons rice vinegar

Grate mouli (white radish) or cut into matchstick strips, place on paper towels and sprinkle with salt. Leave for 30 minutes. Squeeze out any excess moisture, then put mouli (white radish) into a bowl and mix with radishes.

To make the dressing, mix all the ingredients together in a bowl or screw-top jar, then stir into the salad. Spoon salad into a serving dish and serve sprinkled with sesame seeds and garnished with radish leaves.

Serves 6.

CUCUMBER & DILL SALAD

1 large cucumber
salt
4 teaspoons lemon juice or white wine vinegar
black pepper, if desired
1 tablespoon chopped fresh dill

Peel cucumber, reserving a few strips of peel. Cut cucumber in half lengthwise and hollow out the seeds with a teaspoon. Slice thinly, then put into a colander, sprinkle with salt and leave to drain for 30 minutes. Rinse with cold water and dry on paper towels.

    Put cucumber into a bowl and sprinkle with lemon juice or vinegar. Season with pepper, if desired, then stir in dill and serve garnished with strips of cucumber peel.

Serves 4-6.

ARRANGED GREEN SALAD

3 ounces snow peas
8 ounces fresh asparagus, trimmed
2 avocados
watercress sprigs and alfalfa sprouts, to garnish
LIME AND PISTACHIO DRESSING:
grated peel and juice of ½ lime
1 tablespoon virgin olive oil
1 tablespoon sunflower oil
1 ounce shelled pistachio nuts
salt and pepper

Blanch snow peas in a saucepan of boiling water for 30 seconds, drain and dry on paper towels. Cook asparagus in boiling water for 7-8 minutes until tender, then drain and cool.

    Halve avocados, remove seeds and peel. Place, cut side down, on a chopping board and slice crosswise. Gently separate slices and transfer to 4 plates.

    Arrange snow peas and asparagus down either side of avocado. To make the dressing, mix all the ingredients together in a bowl or screw-top jar, then spoon over the salad. Garnish with watercress sprigs and alfalfa sprouts.

Serves 4.

HERB CUCUMBER FRAIS

1 cucumber
1 cup fromage frais
dill sprigs and chive flowers, to garnish
MARINADE:
4 teaspoons chopped fresh tarragon
4 teaspoons chopped fresh dill
4 teaspoons snipped fresh chives
½ teaspoon salt
½ teaspoon black pepper
½ teaspoon dry mustard
2 tablespoons red vermouth

Using a canelle cutter, cut off thin strips of cucumber peel to make a ridge effect. Cut cucumber in half lengthwise, scoop out seeds and cut cucumber into ¼-inch slices.

Bring ⅔ cup water to boil in a pan, add cucumber and cook for 1 minute. Drain.

To make marinade, mix tarragon, dill, chives, salt, pepper, mustard and vermouth together. Add cucumber and turn gently in marinade to coat. Cover with plastic wrap and leave in a cool place for 2 hours.

Just before serving, gently stir in fromage frais until evenly mixed. Place cucumber mixture in a serving dish and garnish with sprigs of dill and chive flowers.

Serves 4.

TOSSED GREEN SALAD

mixture of lettuce to include 2 varieties, such as Cos, Boston, iceberg, Bibb, chicory or batavia
a few young spinach leaves
1 bunch watercress, trimmed
½ cucumber, sliced or diced
1 green pepper, seeded and chopped
2 tablespoons chopped mixed fresh herbs, such as parsley, chervil, tarragon chives
DRESSING:
1 clove garlic
salt
1 tablespoon wine vinegar
2 teaspoons lemon juice
¼ teaspoon Dijon mustard
¼ cup extra-virgin olive oil

Tear salad and spinach leaves into smaller pieces. If not using immediately, place in a plastic bag in the refrigerator.

Make the dressing in a wooden salad bowl. Put garlic and a little salt into bowl and crush to a paste with back of a wooden spoon. Add vinegar, lemon juice and mustard, then stir in oil; continue to mix to make an emulsion.

Add all the salad ingredients to the bowl, toss well so that every leaf is coated with dressing. Serve immediately.

Serves 6 as a side salad.

Note: For a less garlicky flavor, rub the inside of the bowl with a cut clove of garlic, then discard.

If you do not have a wooden salad bowl, the dressing can be made separately and poured over just before serving.

CALIFORNIAN SALAD

| 2 tablespoons unflavored gelatin |
| 4 teaspoons sugar |
| 2 lemons |
| 3 tablespoons wine vinegar |
| few drops yellow food coloring |
| 8 ounces fresh asparagus, cooked |
| 1 large avocado |
| 2 large carrots, grated |
| fresh herbs, to garnish |

Sprinkle gelatin over ⅓ cup water in a small bowl and leave to soften for 2-3 minutes. Stand bowl in a saucepan of hot water and stir until dissolved. Stir in sugar, then set aside to cool.

Grate the peel from 1 of the lemons and squeeze the juice from both. Reserve 1 tablespoon lemon juice. Put the grated peel and remaining juice into a measuring jug and make up to 3¾ cups with water. Add dissolved gelatin, the vinegar and a few drops of yellow food coloring. Pour a little of the liquid into a 7½-cup ring mold and refrigerate until the jelly has set.

Cut the tips off the asparagus and arrange on the set gelatin. Halve avocado, remove seed, peel, then dice flesh. Place in a bowl and mix with reserved lemon juice. Chop asparagus stems and add to the avocado with the carrots. Mix well. Stir in remaining liquid, then spoon into the mold. Refrigerate until set.

To serve, turn out the vegetable ring onto a plate and garnish with herbs.

Serves 8.

SUNSHINE SALAD

| 2 cups carrots, cut into matchstick strips |
| 1 yellow pepper, seeded and cut into thin strips |
| 1 red pepper, seeded and cut into thin strips |
| 1 cup cooked whole corn kernels |
| 1 tablespoon sunflower seeds |
| LEMON MUSTARD VINAIGRETTE: |
| ¼ cup sunflower oil |
| 5 teaspoons lemon juice |
| ½ teaspoon Dijon mustard |
| salt and pepper |

Arrange strips of carrot around the outer edge of a shallow bowl or plate. Place the pepper strips inside this ring in alternate groups. Spoon the corn into the center.

To make the dressing, mix all the ingredients together in a bowl or screw-top jar, then drizzle over the salad. Sprinkle with sunflower seeds just before serving.

Serves 6-8.

FENNEL SALAD

CUCUMBER RAITA

12 radishes
3 fennel bulbs
2 carrots
1 green eating apple
1 tablespoon lemon juice
6 tablespoons mayonnaise

Trim radishes and make vertical cuts on 4 sides. Soak in ice cold water for 2-3 hours until "petals" open. Drain and reserve for garnish.

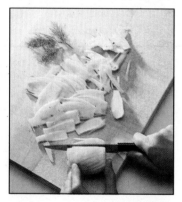

Trim fennel and reserve fern-like tops for garnish. Cut bulbs in half, discarding any hard core. Slice thinly. Peel carrots and cut into thin matchstick strips. Core and dice unpeeled apple. Mix lemon juice into vegetables, then stir in mayonnaise.

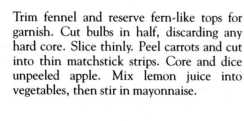

Turn mixed ingredients into a salad bowl and garnish with radish flowers and fennel tops.

Serves 4-6.

Note: Fennel has a strong aniseed flavor and goes particularly well with fish.

1 small cucumber
1 teaspoon salt
2½ cups plain yogurt
1 teaspoon finely chopped onion
1 teaspoon chopped fresh cilantro leaves
pepper
cilantro leaves, to garnish

Peel cucumber and chop finely. Put into a nylon strainer, resting on a thick fold of paper towel. Sprinkle with salt and leave for 1 hour for moisture in cucumber to drain away.

Line another strainer with cheesecloth, place over a bowl and pour in yogurt. Leave in a cool place for 2 hours.

Discard the whey and mix drained yogurt, cucumber, onion and chopped cilantro leaves together. Season to taste with pepper. Transfer to a bowl and garnish with cilantro leaves.

Makes 2 cups.

— SANDWICHES —

CUCUMBER-MINT COOLERS

¼ cucumber, peeled and thinly sliced

½ teaspoon salt

2 teaspoons finely chopped fresh mint

good pinch sugar

¼ teaspoon lemon juice

3 tablespoons butter, softened

4 thin slices whole-wheat or white bread from a small loaf, crusts removed

pepper

mint sprigs, to garnish

Put the cucumber into a strainer and sprinkle with salt, then press down with a saucer and leave to drain for 30 minutes.

Meanwhile, in a bowl, mix mint with sugar, lemon juice and butter until soft and creamy. Butter the slices of bread.

Pat cucumber dry on paper towels and arrange over 2 slices of buttered bread. Season with pepper. Cover with remaining bread slices and press together.

Cut into dainty squares or fingers. Arrange on a serving plate, garnished with sprigs of mint.

Makes 8.

Note: For special occasions, cut sandwiches into dainty shapes using a selection of cookie cutters.

SALMON PINWHEELS

1 large unsliced white sandwich loaf, crusts removed

⅓ cup butter, softened

3 tablespoons finely chopped fresh parsley

1 teaspoon lemon juice

good pinch cayenne pepper

4 ounces thinly sliced smoked salmon

pepper

lemon twists, to garnish

Carefully cut two ¼-inch thick lengthwise slices from the sandwich loaf. Using a rolling pin, roll each slice firmly to flatten.

In a bowl, mix butter with 1 tablespoon parsley, lemon juice and cayenne pepper until well combined. Spread two-thirds of the butter mixture over the slices of bread, reserving a little for later.

Arrange smoked salmon on top of buttered bread and season with pepper. Roll up each slice, like a jelly roll, starting from a short side.

Spread remaining butter all over outside of rolls and coat evenly in remaining chopped parsley.

Wrap rolls tightly in plastic wrap and chill for at least 2 hours. Remove plastic wrap and cut each roll into 7 pinwheels. Arrange on a serving plate, garnished with lemon twists.

Makes 14.

Variation: Coat one whole buttered roll with chopped parsley and the remaining buttered roll in paprika. Chill as above before cutting into pinwheels. Attractively arrange the different rolls on a serving plate.

LOBSTER SANDWICHES

6 ounces cooked lobster, thawed if frozen
and chopped
2 small sticks celery, finely chopped
3 tablespoons mayonnaise
salt
cayenne pepper
¼ cup butter, softened
1 teaspoon lemon juice
1 tablespoon chopped fresh parsley
6 slices pumpernickel
8 thin slices cucumber
8 radishes and 8 small parsley sprigs, to
garnish

Put lobster into a bowl. Add celery and 2 tablespoons mayonnaise. Season with salt and cayenne pepper.

Mix butter with lemon juice and parsley. Using a 2-inch fluted biscuit cutter, cut out 4 circles from each slice of pumpernickel.

Butter 8 pumpernickel circles on one side and remaining 16 on both sides. Cover 8 circles buttered on one side with a slice of cucumber. Top with half the lobster mixture and place half the remaining rounds buttered on both sides on top. Repeat with rest of lobster mixture and bread circles. Press together lightly.

Spread tops lightly with remaining mayonnaise. Cut radishes into dainty wedge-shaped slices and arrange like spokes of a wheel on top of each one. Garnish each sandwich with a small parsley sprig.

Makes 8

Variations: Use flaked white crab meat or chopped cooked shrimp instead of lobster, if preferred.

BRIE & APPLE SLICES

3 tablespoons butter, softened
2 tablespoons chopped walnuts
4 square slices light rye bread, crusts
removed
4 lengthwise slices Brie, about ¼-inch
thick
½ green eating apple
½ red eating apple
1 tablespoon lemon juice
watercress sprigs, to garnish

In a bowl, mix butter with walnuts until thoroughly combined. Spread mixture over the slices of bread.

Cut slices of cheese in half crosswise and arrange 2 pieces on each slice of bread.

Quarter apples and remove cores but do not peel. Slice apples thinly and brush the slices with the lemon juice.

Arrange overlapping alternate slices of green and red apple over cheese. Cut each slice of bread in half diagonally. Arrange on a serving plate, garnished with sprigs of watercress.

Makes 8.

SPICY SHRIMP TEMPTERS

1 cup coarsely chopped shelled shrimp, thawed
2 tablespoons thousand island dressing
2 teaspoons tomato paste
1 teaspoon creamed horseradish sauce
salt and pepper
3 tablespoons butter, softened
4 slices light rye bread, crusts removed
few watercress sprigs
4 small radicchio leaves
watercress sprigs and shelled shrimp (optional), to garnish

In a bowl, mix shrimp with dressing, tomato paste and horseradish sauce, then season with salt and pepper.

Butter slices of bread. Cover 2 slices with watercress sprigs and top with shrimp mixture. Cover with radicchio leaves. Place remaining slices of bread in position, buttered side down.

Press sandwiches together firmly and cut diagonally into quarters. Arrange on a serving plate, garnished with sprigs of watercress and prawns, if desired.

Makes 8.

Variations: Use thinly sliced *daktyla* (Greek sesame seed bread), if preferred, but do not cut off crusts.

Omit radicchio and use crisp green lettuce leaves instead.

PIQUANT SALMON TREATS

6 ounces fresh salmon steak
1 teaspoon lemon juice
salt and pepper
3 tablespoons mayonnaise
1-2 teaspoons capers, drained
3 cocktail gherkins, chopped
1 scallion, chopped
2 lengthwise slices from uncut white sandwich loaf, about ¼-inch thick, crusts removed
3 tablespoons butter, softened
paprika for sprinkling
small parsley sprigs, to garnish

Preheat oven to 350F. Put salmon on a buttered sheet of foil. Sprinkle with lemon juice and season with salt and pepper. Wrap foil to enclose salmon and put on a cookie sheet. Cook for 25 minutes. Cool, then skin and bone.

Flake salmon into a bowl. Add mayonnaise. Dry capers well on paper towels; finely chop. Add capers, gherkins and scallions to bowl. Season with salt and pepper and mix well.

Using a rolling pin, lightly roll slices of bread to flatten slightly. Butter 1 slice on one side and remaining slice on both sides. Using a 2-inch fluted round cookie cutter, cut out 8 circles from slice buttered on one side. Cover these rounds with salmon mixture, reserving a little.

Using same cutter, cut out 8 circles from remaining slice of bread, then, using a small ¾-inch fluted round cutter, cut out center from each circle and discard. Sprinkle circles with paprika and place over salmon. Press lightly. Spoon remaining salmon into centers. Garnish with parsley.

Makes 8.

CHICKEN RELISH SWIRLS

½ cup chopped cooked skinned chicken

2 teaspoons mango chutney, chopped

2 teaspoons mayonnaise

3 tablespoons finely chopped green pepper

2 scallions, finely chopped

2 cocktail gherkins, finely chopped

salt and pepper

3 medium-thick slices white bread, crusts removed

¼ cup butter, softened

about 21 stuffed green olives

cilantro sprigs, to garnish

Purée chicken in a food processor or grind finely. In a bowl, mix chicken and chutney with mayonnaise, green pepper, onions and gherkins. Season with salt and pepper.

Using a rolling pin, roll each slice of bread firmly to flatten. Spread with butter, then spread with chicken mixture.

Arrange a row of stuffed olives along one shorter edge of each slice. Roll up each slice of bread like a jelly roll. Wrap each roll tightly in plastic wrap and chill for at least 2 hours.

Cut each roll at a slight diagonal angle into 7 slices. Arrange slices on a serving plate, garnished with sprigs of cilantro.

Makes 21.

Variations: Use cocktail gherkins to replace stuffed olives.

Use cold cooked turkey instead of chicken, or use a mixture of chicken and ham.

DEVILED CRAB TREATS

4 ounces white crab meat, thawed if frozen and well drained if canned

2 tablespoons mayonnaise

few drops lemon juice

few drops hot-pepper sauce

¼ teaspoon dry mustard

salt and pepper

3 tablespoons butter, softened

4 thin slices whole-wheat or white bread from a small loaf, crusts removed

1-2 crisp lettuce leaves, finely shredded

1 teaspoon paprika

lemon twist and watercress sprigs, to garnish

Flake crab meat into a bowl. Add all but 1 teaspoon mayonnaise, lemon juice, hot-pepper sauce and mustard. Season with salt and pepper, then mix together lightly.

Butter slices of bread. Spread 2 slices with crab mixture and top with shredded lettuce. Cover with remaining slices of buttered bread. Press together firmly and cut diagonally into quarters.

Hold each sandwich by the long straight edge and very lightly spread reserved mayonnaise on to one alternate edge of each sandwich. Dip these coated edges into paprika.

Arrange sandwiches on a serving plate, standing them in rows of 4 with pointed ends upward. Garnish with a lemon twist and sprigs of watercress.

Makes 8.

Variations: Use peeled and thinly sliced cucumber instead of finely shredded lettuce.

Coat edges in finely chopped chives instead of paprika, or for a colorful combination, coat half in paprika and remainder in chives.

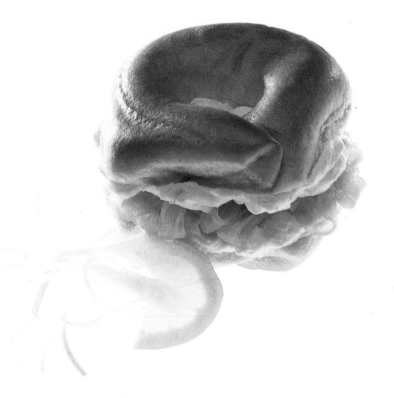

SMOKED SALMON BAGELS

2 bagels
6 ounces cream cheese
2 teaspoons lemon juice
2 tablespoons thick soured cream
3 scallions, chopped
a little cayenne pepper
2-3 ounces thinly sliced smoked
salmon
scallons flowers and lemon twists, to
garnish

Preheat oven to 350F. Wrap bagels in foil and heat in oven for 15 minutes.

Meanwhile, in a bowl, mix together cheese, lemon juice, soured cream and scallions and season with cayenne pepper. Form smoked salmon into rolls and cut into thin slices.

Cut warmed bagels in half. Spread the bases with half of the cheese mixture. Arrange smoked salmon slices over bases, cover with remaining cheese mixture and sandwich bagels together with top halves. Garnish with scallions flowers and lemon twists.

Makes 2.

PORK & CELERY CRUNCH

1 tablespoon mayonnaise
1 teaspoon French mustard
1 stick celery, chopped
1-2 teaspoons applesauce (optional)
salt and pepper
2 tablespoons butter, softened
2 large chunky slices whole-wheat bread
1 chunky slice iceberg lettuce
2-3 slices cooked roast pork
a few red onion rings
small leafy sticks celery and red onion
rings, to garnish

In a bowl, mix mayonnaise with mustard, celery and applesauce, if desired. Season with salt and pepper.

Butter slices of bread. Arrange lettuce slice on 1 slice of bread. Add slices of pork, folded over to fit neatly, and spoon celery mixture over pork. Cover with onion rings.

Place remaining slice of bread on top. Press together lightly and cut diagonally into quarters. Garnish with small leafy sticks celery and red onion rings.

Makes 4.

Variation: Omit pork and applesauce and replace with cold roast beef or corned beef and horseradish sauce, if preferred.

SCOTCH EGG ROLLS

8 ounces pork sausage-meat
1 small onion, finely chopped
salt and pepper
2 hard-boiled eggs, shelled
1 tablespoon flour
1 egg, beaten
3 tablespoons dry bread crumbs
vegetable oil for deep frying
4 rolls
1/3 cup butter, softened
curly chicory leaves
2 large tomatoes, thinly sliced
2 tablespoons piccalilli or other relish
TO GARNISH:
curly chicory sprigs
crisp bacon rolls
radish flowers

Put sausage-meat and onion in a bowl. Season with salt and pepper and mix well. Divide in half. Roll hard-boiled eggs in flour and, with lightly floured hands, wrap eggs in sausagemeat mixture to enclose completely. Smooth over joins, then dip in beaten egg and roll in bread crumbs, pressing on firmly.

Half fill a deep-fat fryer or pan with oil and heat to 375F or until a cube of day-old bread browns in 40 seconds. Fry eggs 6 minutes until golden. Drain and cool.

Cut off top portions of rolls and spread with butter. Cut a thin slice from base of rolls and spread each cut side with butter. Scoop out soft bread from center sections of rolls, large enough to take a halved Scotch egg. Spread with butter.

Cover base slices with chicory and tomato. Place center sections on top. Cut eggs in half, press into holes in rolls and top with piccalilli. Add lids at an angle and secure with cocktail sticks threaded with chicory, bacon rolls and radishes.

Makes 4.

TUNA-AVOCADO SANDWICHES

3½-ounce can tuna in oil, drained
2 scallions, chopped
2 tablespoons tartare sauce
salt and pepper
1 ripe avocado
1 tablespoon lemon juice
1/4 cup butter, softened
4 slices light rye bread
TO GARNISH:
small wedges of lemon
avocado slices
parsley sprigs

Flake tuna into a bowl. Add scallions and 1 tablespoon tartare sauce. Season to taste with salt and pepper and mix well together.

Halve avocado and remove seed. Peel avocado and cut into slices, then dip in lemon juice.

Butter slices of bread. Cover 2 slices with tuna mixture and top with avocado slices. Spread with remaining tartare sauce and season with salt and pepper.

Cover with remaining bread slices and press together firmly. Cut diagonally into halves. Garnish with small wedges of lemon, avocado slices and sprigs of parsley.

Makes 4.

PÂTÉ & SALAD CROISSANTS

2 croissants
2 tablespoons butter, softened
1½ ounces Boursin cheese
6 small lettuce leaves
6 large slices tomato, halved
4 ounces firm pâté, sliced
salt and pepper
TO GARNISH:
2 crisp bacon rolls
2 black olives
2 small lettuce leaves

Cut croissants two-thirds way through centers, cutting from rounded sides through to pointed sides but do not cut right through. Open out slightly and spread both sides lightly with butter.

Spread one side with Boursin cheese and add lettuce leaves, set at an angle. Add 3 tomato slices to each croissant and arrange slices of pâté along one side. Place remaining halves of tomato slices along other side of pâté and season with salt and pepper.

To garnish, thread bacon rolls, olives and small lettuce leaves on to 2 cocktail sticks and secure one into each croissant.

Makes 2.

Variations: Top filled croissants with a little mayonnaise or pickle of your choice, if wished.

STILTON-PEAR TOPPER

1½ teaspoons unsalted butter, softened
1 slice crusty whole-wheat bread
few chicory sprigs
½ ripe pear, cored and sliced
1 teaspoon lemon juice
2 slices Stilton cheese
1 walnut half
lemon twist and 2 small watercress sprigs, to garnish

Spread butter over the slice of bread. Place chicory sprigs over buttered bread and press down.

Brush slices of pear with lemon juice. Place slices of cheese on bread and arrange slices of pear in an overlapping fan-shape to one side of cheese.

Add the walnut half and garnish with a lemon twist and small sprigs of watercress.

Makes 1.

Variations: Use Danish blue, Cambozola, Dolcelatte or Roquefort cheese instead of Stilton. Replace pear slices with slices of star fruit.

POTTED SHRIMP TREAT

3 tablespoons unsalted butter, plus
1½ teaspoons for spreading
⅓ cup coarsely chopped shelled shrimps,
see Note
½ small clove garlic, crushed
pinch ground cumin
pinch ground mace
2 pinches cayenne pepper
1 teaspoon finely chopped fresh parsley
salt and white pepper
1 slice pumpernickel
3-4 small radicchio leaves
TO GARNISH:
several flat-leaved parsley sprigs
shelled or unshelled shrimps

Melt 1 tablespoon butter in a sauce-pan. Add shrimps and garlic and cook gently for 1 minute. Remove from heat and stir in cumin, mace, cayenne pepper and parsley. Season with salt and white pepper and mix well. Spoon into a ½ cup capacity ramekin and level surface.

Melt 2 tablespoons remaining butter in a pan, then cool slightly. Pour over shrimp mixture. Cool, then chill for 2 hours or until set.

Spread remaining butter over pumpernickel and top with radicchio leaves. Run a knife around edges of ramekin to loosen shrimp mold and turn out. Place mold in center of sandwich and surround with sprigs of flat-leaved parsley. Garnish with shrimps.

Makes 1.

Note: If using thawed frozen shrimp, the thawed weight should be 2 ounces. Squeeze thawed shrimp in paper towels to remove excess moisture.

SPICED EGG SLICE

1 hard-boiled egg, shelled and chopped
1 tablespoon mayonnaise
¼ cup finely diced cheddar cheese
1 scallion, chopped
½-¾ teaspoon concentrated curry paste
salt and pepper
1½ teaspoons butter, softened
1 slice pumpernickel
16 cucumber slices
3 small radish flowers and mint sprigs, to garnish

In a bowl, mix together hard-boiled egg, mayonnaise, cheese, scallion and curry paste. Season with salt and pepper.

Spread butter over slice of pumpernickel. Arrange overlapping slices of cucumber all the way around edges, allowing slices to slightly overlap edges of bread.

Spoon curried egg mixture into center and level slightly to neaten and to cover inner edges of cucumber slices. Garnish with radish flowers and sprigs of mint.

Makes 1.

Variations: Use thick soured cream instead of mayonnaise and 1 table-spoon snipped fresh chives instead of scallion.

BEEF & ENDIVE CRUNCH

1½ teaspoons unsalted butter,
softened

1 slice pumpernickel

4-5 endive leaves

1 teaspoon mayonnaise

1 teaspoon creamed horseradish sauce

2 slices rare roast beef

1 tablespoon pickled red cabbage, drained

dill sprigs and cucumber twists, to garnish

Spread butter over the slice of
pumpernickel. Arrange endive
leaves at an angle over bread.

Mix mayonnaise with horseradish sauce and spread over slices
of beef. Fold beef slices and arrange
over endive. Spoon red cabbage on
to sandwich. Garnish with sprigs
of dill and cucumber twists.

Makes 1.

Variations: Use slices of cooked
ham instead of rare beef. Finely
shredded radicchio leaves, tossed in
la vingarette dressing, make a
tasty change from pickled red
cabbage.

CHILIED SALAMI HERO

½ small French stick, or large, long
whole-wheat roll

3 tablespoons butter, softened

1 small clove garlic, crushed

1-2 tablespoons chopped canned green
chili

½ ripe avocado

1 teaspoon lemon juice

4 slices salami, rinded

1 slice processed cheddar cheese, cut
diagonally into quarters

cherry tomatoes and pickled whole
chilies, to garnish (optional)

Cut French stick or roll lengthwise
two-thirds way up from base, but do
not cut right through. Open out roll
sufficiently to take the filling. In a
bowl, mix butter with garlic and
spread over roll. Sprinkle base with
chopped chili.

Peel avocado and cut into slices,
then dip in lemon juice. Arrange
along base of roll to create a fan-
shape. Fold slices of salami into
quarters and arrange over avocado.
Arrange cheese slices on top of
salami.

Garnish with 2 or 3 cocktail
sticks, threaded with cherry
tomatoes and pickled chilies, if
desired.

Makes 1.

CHEESE & HAM ROLL-UPS

1 short sesame-seeded French stick
1/4 cup butter, softened
1 teaspoon mustard
2-3 tablespoons mayonnaise
3 square slices cooked ham
1 1/3 cups ricotta cheese
1 carton cress
salt and pepper
18 slices cucumber
3 small tomatoes, thinly sliced
6 watercress sprigs, to garnish

Cut out 6 "V" shaped pieces at regular intervals along French stick, each deep and wide enough to hold a stuffed ham roll plus cucumber and tomato slices along each edge.

Mix butter with mustard and spread over "V" shapes, then spread with mayonnaise.

Spread ham slices with ricotta cheese. Arrange cress, green parts facing outward, along 2 opposite edges and season with salt and pepper. Roll up ham to show green cress at either end. Carefully cut each ham roll in half to make 6 small rolls.

Place overlapping cucumber and tomato slices along the edges of each "V" shaped cut.

Place a ham roll in each "V" shape
and garnish each one with a watercress sprig. Serve cut into chunk slices.

Makes 6.

SAUCY SEAFOOD LOAF

1 short French stick
1/3 cup butter
1 onion, finely chopped
1/2 cup flour
1 1/4 cups milk
1/2 cup light cream
2 tablespoons dry white wine
6 ounces shelled cooked shrimps
6 ounce salmon steak, cooked
2 tablespoons chopped fresh parsley
salt and pepper
1/4 cup grated Emmental or cheddar cheese
lemon slices and shelled shrimp and parsley, to garnish

Preheat oven to 375F. Cut loaf centrally along top but do not cut right through. Open out slightly and pull out soft bread from both sides, leaving shell intact. Make about 3/4 cup bread crumbs.

Melt 1/4 cup butter in a saucepan, add onion and fry for 3 minutes. Stir in flour and cook for 1 minute, then gradually stir in milk and cream and bring to a boil, stirring. Simmer for 2 minutes. Add wine, shrimps, salmon and parsley. Season with salt and pepper.

Spoon mixture into French stick and place on a sheet of foil on a cookie sheet. Melt remaining butter in a pan, remove from heat and add bread crumbs. Mix well, then sprinkle over filling in French stick. Sprinkle with cheese. Wrap foil around sides of loaf, leaving top exposed.

Cook for 20-25 minutes until topping is golden. Garnish with lemon slices, shrimps and parsley. Cut into 4 and serve hot.

Serves 4.

CHICKEN MARYLAND ROLLS

4 crusty poppy seed knot-shaped rolls
1/3 cup butter, softened
2 skinned chicken breast fillets
salt and pepper
1/2 cup plain flour
1 egg
1 tablespoon milk
2 scallions, chopped
2 potatoes, grated
4 tablespoons corn kernels, drained if canned and thawed if frozen
vegetable oil for frying
2 small bananas
a little shredded lettuce
a little tomato relish
2 tomatoes, thinly sliced
watercress sprigs, to garnish

Cut the rolls in half and spread with 1/4 cup butter. Cut each chicken breast into 4 thin slices by cutting at an angle through each. Season with salt and pepper.

In a bowl, mix flour with egg and milk. Add onions, potatoes and corn. Season and mix well. Heat oil in a large skillet. Divide corn mixture into 4 and press out in pan into circles the same size as rolls. Fry for 6 minutes, turning once, until golden. Drain and keep warm.

Pour off oil from pan. Add remaining butter to pan and fry chicken for 2-3 minutes on each side. Drain and keep warm. Cut bananas in half crosswise and then in half lengthwise. Add to pan and fry for 30-45 seconds.

Arrange a little lettuce on rolls; spread with relish and top each with a corn fritter. Add slices of tomato, 2 slices of chicken and 2 slices of banana to each one.

Secure lids in position with cocktail sticks and garnish with sprigs of watercress.

Makes 4.

STUFFED FRENCH STICK

1 cup chopped sliced garlic sausage
1/2 cup chopped salted cashews
4 scallions, chopped
1 small green pepper, seeded and chopped
2 sticks celery, chopped
8 ounces cream cheese with chives
4 teaspoons tomato paste
1 clove garlic, crushed
salt and pepper
1 short whole-wheat French stick
scallion flowers and small tomato water lilies, to garnish

In a bowl, mix together garlic sausage, nuts, onions, green pepper, celery, cream cheese, tomato paste and garlic. Season with salt and pepper and mix well.

Cut French stick in half cross-wise. Cut crusty ends off French stick pieces and, using a sharp, pointed knife, cut away soft bread from inside each piece, leaving crust intact.

Using a teaspoon, fill centers of French stick with cream cheese mixture, pushing in well from both ends to prevent any gaps in filling.

Wrap in foil and chill for 2 hours. Cut each piece into 10 slices and garnish with scallion flowers and tomato water lilies.

Makes 20.

Variations: Use any flavor cream cheese of your choice, or use fromage frais, if preferred.

DESSERTS

GRAND MARNIER KABOBS

PRALINE BANANAS

3 firm apricots
3 firm fresh figs
two 1-inch thick trimmed pineapple slices
2 satsumas
2 firm bananas
2 eating apples
1 tablespoon lemon juice
⅓ cup unsalted butter
½ cup confectioners' sugar
1 tablespoon Grand Marnier
1 tablespoon fresh orange juice
1 tablespoon finely grated orange peel

Halve apricots and remove seeds. Remove stems and quarter figs lengthwise.

Remove any woody core and cut pineapple slices into chunks. Peel satsumas and quarter but do not remove membranes. Peel bananas and cut into 1-inch thick slices. Peel apples, cut into quarters, remove cores and halve each apple piece crosswise. Sprinkle apples and bananas with lemon juice to prevent discoloration.

Thread fruit onto 6-8 skewers, making sure that each has a mixture of fruit and starting and finishing with apple and pineapple. Melt butter, stir in confectioners' sugar, then add Grand Marnier, orange juice and peel. Brush kabobs with sauce and barbecue over medium coals for 5-6 minutes, frequently basting with sauce. Serve any remaining sauce with kabobs. Serve hot.

Serves 6-8.

1 tablespoon unskinned almonds
1 tablespoon unskinned hazelnuts
¼ cup sugar
6 under-ripe bananas
whipped cream, to serve

Put almonds, hazelnuts and sugar in a small, heavy-based skillet. Heat gently, stirring constantly until sugar dissolves. Raise heat and cook to a deep brown syrup. Immediately, pour on to a sheet of non-stick paper placed on a cookie sheet on a wooden board. The toffee-like mixture will be very hot. Leave until cold and brittle; crush finely.

Lay unpeeled bananas flat and make a slit through the skin along top surface. Slightly open out the skin and fill each slit with about 3 teaspoons of praline. Re-shape the bananas and wrap individually and tightly in double thickness foil, sealing along the top.

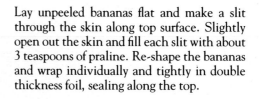

Barbecue directly on medium coals for 8-10 minutes, turning packets over halfway through cooking time. To serve, unfold foil wrapping and slightly open banana skins. Serve with whipped cream.

Serves 6.

PEACHES & BUTTERSCOTCH

6 peaches
angelica, to decorate, if desired

BUTTERSCOTCH SAUCE: ½ cup light soft brown sugar
⅔ cup maple syrup
3 tablespoons butter
pinch of salt
⅔ cup light cream
few drops vanilla extract

FILLING: ½ cup blanched almonds, ground
2 tablespoons finely chopped angelica

Wash, dry and halve peaches; remove seeds.

To make sauce, combine sugar, maple syrup, butter and salt in a heavy-based saucepan. Bring to a boil, stir once, then boil for 3 minutes to form a thick syrup. Stir in cream, bring back to a boil and immediately remove from heat. Stir in vanilla extract to taste. Pour into a large measuring jug and keep warm.

Put peach halves, cut-sides down, on individual squares of double thickness foil. Curl up sides of foil but do not seal. Barbecue on rack over hot coals for 5 minutes. Turn peaches over on the foil; spoon almonds and angelica into cavities and pour over a tablespoon of butterscotch sauce. Draw up edges of foil and twist above peaches to seal. Barbecue for 10 minutes until tender. Decorate with angelica, if desired, and serve hot with remaining sauce.

Serves 6-12.

VODKA-SOUSED PINEAPPLE

4 large, fresh ¾-inch thick pineapple slices
3 tablespoons vodka
⅓ cup unsalted butter
¼ cup heavy cream
1 teaspoon ground cardamom
2 tablespoons confectioners' sugar
12 bottled morello cherries
confectioners' sugar for dusting

Peel pineapple and remove central core. Pour vodka into a shallow dish, add pineapple slices, then turn slices over once. Cover dish and leave to marinate for 20 minutes.

Melt butter in a small saucepan. Stir in cream, cardamom and confectioners' sugar.

Dip pineapple slices into melted butter mixture and barbecue on rack over hot coals for 5 minutes on each side until golden brown. Serve on warm plates, with pineapple centers filled with morello cherries. Dust lightly with confectioners' sugar.

Serves 4.

RUM & RAISIN SHARON FRUIT

HOT TROPICANAS

6 firm sharon fruit
2 tablespoons mixed dried fruit
1 candied cherry
3 unskinned almonds
2 teaspoons dark soft brown sugar
1 teaspoon dark rum
pinch of ground cinnamon
½ teaspoon lemon juice
6 small strawberries

Remove stems from sharon fruit and, using a teaspoon, scoop out pulp, leaving fleshy wall intact. Put pulp in a bowl.

Using a sharp, lightly floured knife, very finely chop dried fruit, cherry and almonds. Mix into fruit pulp, adding sugar, rum, cinnamon and lemon juice. Carefully pack filling into sharon shells and wrap separately in lightly oiled, double thickness foil.

Place foil packages in medium coals and cook for 25-30 minutes until fruit is soft. To serve, unwrap and top each one with a strawberry.

Serves 6.

3 pink grapefruit
8 lychees
2 kumquats, rinsed and dried
1 guava
1 pawpaw
1 small mango
4 tablespoons maple syrup
2 tablespoons butter
2 tablespoons shredded coconut, toasted

Halve grapefruit, separate and remove segments and drain. Scrape out grapefruit shells, discarding membranes.

Peel and pit lychees. Slice kumquats. Halve guava and pawpaw. Scoop out seeds, then peel and dice flesh. Peel mango, pare flesh away from stone and cut into strips. Combine all fruits in a bowl. Melt syrup, pour over fruits and mix gently.

Spoon into grapefruit shells. Top each with a small knob of butter. Wrap grapefruit in large individual pieces of double thickness foil and barbecue on rack over medium coals for 7-10 minutes until fruit is warm but not cooked. Remove grapefruit from foil, place in individual dishes and top with toasted coconut.

Serves 6.

Note: Decorate the grapefruit with sprigs of mint, if desired.

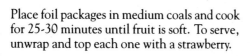

PEAR & PEACH APPLES

2 dried pear halves
2 dried peach halves
1 tablespoon golden raisins
good pinch of ground cloves
pinch of apple pie spice
1/3 cup light soft brown sugar
2 tablespoons butter
4 cooking apples
whipped cream, to serve

Put pear and peach halves in a saucepan. Add sufficient water to just cover fruits, then bring to a boil and cook for 5 minutes. Drain thoroughly, then chop. Mix with golden raisins, spices, sugar and butter.

Wash and core apples. Put on individual squares of double thickness foil. Stuff cavities with fruit filling, packing it in firmly. Draw up edges of foil and twist firmly to secure over apples.

Barbecue on rack over medium coals for 45-50 minutes. Using twisted foil as an aid, turn apples on their sides from time to time. Alternatively, cook directly in coals without turning for 20-30 minutes. To serve, snip off foil stems and fold foil back to expose apples. Serve with whipped cream.

Serves 4.

KIWIS & STEM GINGER

6 pieces preserved stem ginger in syrup
6 firm kiwi fruit, unpeeled
5-6 tablespoons preserved stem ginger syrup
2/3 cup whipping cream
3 teaspoons confectioners' sugar
1 tablespoon chopped shelled pistachio nuts

Cut pieces of stem ginger in half lengthwise. Rinse and dry kiwi fruit and halve lengthwise. Remove firm cores, chop and reserve. Spoon a little ginger syrup over kiwi flesh and pierce with a skewer to help absorption. Stiffly whip cream with sugar and refrigerate until required.

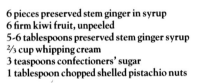

Place the ginger in cavities in kiwi fruit. Place filled kiwi halves, skin-sides down, on to squares of foil and pour a little more ginger syrup over ginger. Wrap up securely.

Barbecue over medium hot coals for 10-15 minutes, turning packages over toward end of cooking time. Serve in open packages, cut-sides of fruit uppermost. Sprinkle with nuts and reserved chopped cores. Serve with the sweetened whipped cream.

Serves 6.

Note: This dish can also be served as an appetizer – in which case omit the cream and sugar.

BRANDIED FRUIT CRÊPES

¾ cup superfine sugar	
4 strips pared lemon peel	
4 ounces kumquats	
3 nectarines, sliced	
butter for frying	
¼ cup apricot brandy	
mint leaves or tiny flowers, to decorate	
BATTER:	
1 cup flour	
⅔ cup milk	
1 egg	

Gently heat sugar, lemon peel and 1¼ cups water in a saucepan until sugar has dissolved. Add kumquats and bring to the a boil, then cover and cook gently for 5 minutes.

Pour kumquats into a bowl, add nectarines and set aside until cold.

Meanwhile, to make batter, place flour in a bowl and mix milk and egg together with ⅔ cup water in a measuring jug, beating until well blended. Make a well in center of flour and add half milk mixture, beating well with a wooden spoon. Add remaining milk, beating well.

Melt enough butter to lightly grease a small skillet. Pour in enough batter to just thinly coat base of pan and swirl pan to spread the batter. Cook for about 1 minute on each side.

Place crêpe on a plate covered with paper towel; repeat to make 10-12 crêpes. Cover and keep warm.

Strain syrup from fruit into a saucepan, boil rapidly for 3-4 minutes, until thick. Cool slightly, stir in brandy and pour over fruit.

Fold crêpes into 4 making a triangle and serve with kumquats, nectarines and syrup. Decorate with mint leaves or tiny flowers.

Serves 4.

FIG & PORT ICE CREAM

½ cup superfine sugar	
⅔ cup ruby port	
1½-inch cinnamon stick	
6 fresh figs	
4 teaspoons freshly squeezed lime juice	
1¼ cups heavy cream	
fresh fig slices and mint leaves, to decorate	

Place sugar and port in a saucepan and heat gently, stirring occasionally, until sugar has melted. Bring to a boil, then add cinnamon stick and figs, cover and cook very gently for 5 minutes. Leave the figs in the marinade, still covered, until they are completely cold.

Transfer figs and liquid to a food processor and process until smooth.

Pour mixture into a strainer over a bowl and rub through using a wooden spoon. Stir in lime juice.

Whip cream until thick, then fold into fig purée until evenly blended. Pour mixture into a plastic container, cover and freeze for 1-2 hours, until almost frozen.

Return mixture to food processor and process until thick and smooth. Return to plastic container and freeze until firm. Scoop ice cream to serve, then decorate.

Serves 4.

FRUIT KABOBS

4 teaspoons dark rum or sherry
¼ cup sugar
½ fresh pineapple, flesh cut into bite-size pieces with juice reserved
2 oranges, peeled with all white pith removed and segmented with juice reserved
2 nectarines, sliced
24 cherries, stoned
2 bananas, sliced
2 teaspoons lemon juice
2 teaspoons ground cinnamon
⅔ cup heavy cream

Mix rum and half the sugar together in a large bowl. Add pineapple and oranges with any reserved juices and nectarines and cherries.

Toss banana slices in lemon juice to prevent discoloration, then add to bowl; turn fruit in marinade to coat evenly. Cover with plastic wrap and leave for 15 minutes.

Mix together remaining sugar and cinnamon on a flat plate. Fill 6 thin wooden skewers with a mixture of fruit.

Roll each kabob in the sugar and cinnamon mixture to coat evenly. Whip cream until thick, add remaining marinade juices and fold in carefully until well blended. Place in a serving bowl.

Prepare barbecue or preheat broiler. Cook kabobs for 2-3 minutes, turning once, until hot and tinged with brown. Serve with the cream.

Serves 6.

MIXED FRUIT TARTLETS

2 figs, sliced
8 teaspoons black currants
3 ounces green grapes
1 peach, peeled and sliced
½ cup cream cheese
⅔ cup plain yogurt
1 teaspoon arrowroot
SWEET PASTRY:
1 cup flour
⅓ cup butter, chilled and diced
2 tablespoons superfine sugar
1 egg yolk
MARINADE:
8 teaspoons grenadine syrup
8 teaspoons white wine or cider
6 teaspoons chopped fresh apple mint or other mint

To make pastry, put flour in a mixing bowl and cut in butter until mixture resembles bread crumbs. Stir in sugar and egg yolk and mix to a soft dough. Wrap in plastic wrap and chill for 30 minutes.

To make marinade, mix grenadine, wine or cider and mint together in a bowl. Add fig slices, black currants, grapes and peach. Turn to coat with marinade. Cover with plastic wrap and chill.

Preheat oven to 375F. Roll out dough thinly and line 8 individual brioche molds or tartlet pans. Prick dough with a fork and chill until firm. Bake for 8-10 minutes, until pastry is pale in color. Cool in pan for 5 minutes, then turn out onto a wire rack.

Mix cream cheese and yogurt together. Strain marinade from fruit into a small saucepan, blend in arrowroot and bring to a boil, stirring. Cook for 30 seconds; cool.

Fill each tartlet with cream cheese mixture and fruit and glaze with marinade.

Makes 8.

JEWELED FRUIT JELLY

2 cups red grape juice	
2 cups white grape juice	
2 tablespoons unflavored gelatin	
1 star fruit, sliced	
²⁄₃ cup white seedless grapes	
²⁄₃ cup pitted cherries	
²⁄₃ cup halved and sliced strawberries	
strawberry leaves and flowers, to decorate	
MARINADE:	
4 teaspoons orange flower water or Cointreau	
4 teaspoons rosewater or kirsch	
8 teaspoons confectioners' sugar	

Pour red and white grape juices into separate bowls. Sprinkle gelatin over ⅓ cup water in a bowl and stir. Dissolve over a pan of hot water until clear, then stir half into each bowl of juice.

To make marinade, pour flower water or Cointreau, and rosewater or kirsch on to separate plates; sift half the confectioners' sugar on to each. Add star fruit and grapes to flower water or Cointreau, and cherries and strawberries to rose-water or kirsch. Cover and leave 30 minutes.

Using a 6-cup fluted mold or 8 individual molds, pour ½ inch white juice into mold. Cool until just setting.

Arrange one-third star fruit and grapes over gelatin, spoon over white juice to cover; leave until set.

Arrange one-third cherries and strawberries over white gelatin layer, then cover with red juice and leave to set. Repeat layering until all fruit and juices have been used. Leave for 1 hour until jelly has set.

Dip mold into hand-hot water for 1-2 seconds, then invert on to a serving plate. Decorate with extra fruit or leaves and flowers.

Serves 8.

FRUIT CHEESE DESSERT

¼ cup Marsala	
¼ teaspoon ground mace	
1 cup chopped mixed candied fruit	
1½ cups ricotta or cream cheese	
4 teaspoons sugar	
2 eggs, separated	
2 teaspoons grated lemon peel	
²⁄₃ cup whipping cream	
fresh or candied fruit and mint leaves, to decorate	

Mix Marsala, mace and candied fruit together in a bowl, stirring until well blended. Cover with plastic wrap and leave for several hours.

Put ricotta or cream cheese into a bowl, add sugar, egg yolks and lemon peel, beating with a wooden spoon until smooth. Add marinated fruit and stir until well mixed with the cheese.

Whisk egg whites; whip cream until it peaks softly. Fold alternately into cheese mixture.

Spoon into 6 small dishes and chill for 1 hour before serving. Decorate top of each dessert with fresh or candied fruit and a mint leaf.

Serves 6.

ROSE PETAL PAVLOVAS

3 egg whites
1 cup superfine sugar
1 teaspoon rosewater
1 teaspoon raspberry vinegar
1 teaspoon cornstarch
rose pink food coloring
½ cup raspberries
½ cup hulled and sliced strawberries
⅔ cup red currants or pitted cherries
1¼ cups heavy cream
½ cup thick plain yogurt
rose petals for decoration
MARINADE:
4 teaspoons rosewater
4 teaspoons rosé wine
8 teaspoons confectioners' sugar, sifted
petals from 2 scented roses

Preheat oven to 250F. Line 2 cookie sheets with waxed paper.

Beat egg whites until stiff, then add sugar a little at a time, beating well after each addition, until thick. Mix rosewater, vinegar, cornstarch and a drop of pink food coloring together. Add to meringue and beat until thick and glossy.

Place 12 dessertspoonfuls of meringue, spaced apart, onto a cookie sheet. Bake for 45 minutes. Turn off oven and leave until cold.

To make marinade, mix rosewater, rosé wine, confectioners' sugar and rose petals together. Add fruit and turn carefully to coat evenly. Cover with plastic wrap and chill for 30 minutes.

Whip cream until thick, fold in yogurt and strain in marinade.

Arrange pavlovas on a serving plate, spoon cream onto each, top with fruit and decorate with petals.

Makes 12.

TIPSY FRUIT CLOUD

2 kiwi fruit, peeled and cubed
2 peaches, peeled, stoned and cubed
½ pineapple, peeled, cored and cubed
1 cup hulled strawberries
½ cup fromage frais
½ cup heavy cream
mint leaves, to decorate
MARINADE
1 tablespoon dark rum
1 tablespoon kirsch
1 tablespoon peach brandy
½ cup confectioners' sugar, sifted
2 teaspoons finely grated orange peel

To make marinade, mix rum, kirsch, brandy, confectioners' sugar and orange peel together in a shallow dish.

Add all fruit to marinade and turn carefully to coat evenly. Cover with plastic wrap and chill for 1-2 hours to marinate.

Whip fromage frais and cream together until thick. Strain marinade from mixed fruit into a bowl. Reserve a few pieces of fruit for decoration and carefully fold remaining fruit into cream mixture.

Divide fruit between 6 glasses and decorate with fresh mint leaves and top with reserved fruit. Serve the marinade as a sauce.

Serves 6.

CHERRY CHEESE STRUDEL

¾ cup ricotta cheese

½ cup cottage cheese

¼ cup soured cream

3 tablespoons blanched almonds

1 cup butter

2 cups fresh bread crumbs

8 sheets phyllo pastry

12-ounce can black cherries

⅓ cup dark soft brown sugar

TO SERVE:

confectioners' sugar

light cream

Preheat oven to 400F. In a bowl, beat cheeses and soured cream. Stir in almonds. In a large skillet, melt ⅓ cup of the butter and fry bread crumbs until golden.

Spread a clean dish towel on a table and dust with flour. Melt remaining butter in a saucepan. Place sheet of pastry on dish towel and brush with melted butter. Cover with a second sheet of pastry and continue until pastry and most of the butter are used up. Spread cheese mixture over two-thirds of the pastry.

Drain cherries and arrange on cheese. Sprinkle fried bread crumbs and brown sugar over cherries. Using the dish towel, roll up filling and pastry into a long sausage. Brush pastry with remaining melted butter. Bake for 40 minutes until golden and serve with cream.

Serves 8.

BLACKBERRY CHEESECAKE

½ cup butter

2 tablespoons light soft brown sugar

2 cups rolled oats

FILLING:

1 pound ricotta cheese

⅔ cup soured cream

⅓ cup superfine sugar

2 eggs

1 tablespoon flour

pinch of ground cloves

1 pound cooking apples

½ cup blackberries, thawed if frozen

TOPPING:

2 cups blackberries, thawed if frozen

¼ cup red-currant jelly

⅔ cup whipping cream

10 sprigs of mint

Preheat oven to 350F. Grease and line an 8-inch round, loose-bottomed cake pan. In a saucepan, melt butter, then stir in brown sugar and oats. Mix well, then press into cake pan.

In a bowl, beat cheese, soured cream, sugar and eggs. Add flour and cloves and beat until smooth. Peel, core and chop apples. Stir into cheese with the ½ cup blackberries. Spoon on to base and bake in the oven before removing from pan.

To make topping, arrange blackberries in center of cheesecake. Melt red-currant jelly in a small saucepan, then brush over blackberries. Whip cream and pipe a border of 10 rosettes around edge of cheesecake. Top each rosette with a mint sprig.

Serves 8–10.

RHUBARB & CUSTARD CAKE

½ cup butter	
1¼ cups ginger cookie crumbs	
FILLING:	
2 tablespoons cornstarch	
1 cup milk	
3 egg yolks	
few drops vanilla extract	
4 teaspoons unflavored gelatin	
12 ounces medium-fat soft cheese	
TOPPING:	
2 pounds rhubarb	
⅓ cup sugar	
2½ cups boiling water	

Grease a 9-inch round, loose-bottomed cake pan. In a saucepan, melt butter, then stir in cookie crumbs. Mix well, then press into base of cake pan.

In a heatproof bowl, mix cornstarch with 3 tablespoons milk. Add egg yolks and vanilla extract. Stir well. In a saucepan, bring remaining milk to a boil. Pour into bowl and stir well, then pour back into saucepan and simmer to thicken.

Sprinkle gelatin over 2 table-spoons water in a small bowl and leave to soften for 2–3 minutes. Stir into custard and leave to cool.

Put cheese in a bowl. When custard has cooled and nearly set, blend a little at a time into cheese. Pour on to cookie base and leave to set in the refrigerator for 2–3 hours.

Meanwhile, prepare topping. Cut rhubarb into 2½-inch slices. Arrange in a baking dish, sprinkle over sugar and pour over boiling water. Cover and leave to cook in its own heat for 25–30 minutes.

When cheesecake has set, remove from pan. Remove rhubarb from liquid and drain on a wire rack. Arrange pieces in a fan shape around edge of cheesecake. Chill until ready to serve.

Serves 8.

CAROUSEL DE FROMAGE

1 pound medium-fat soft cheese	
1¼ cups whipping cream	
⅓ cup sugar	
3 eggs	
few drops vanilla extract	
TO DECORATE:	
2 eating apples	
2 pears	
1 cup strawberries	
1 cup raspberries	
⅔ cup black grapes	
2 oranges	
1 kiwi fruit	
⅔ cup whipping cream	
10 sprigs of mint	

Preheat oven to 375F. Grease a 9-inch ring mold. In a bowl, beat cheese and cream until smooth. Add sugar, eggs and vanilla extract and blend evenly. Spoon into ring mold.

Stand ring mold in a roasting pan and add enough boiling water to come halfway up sides of ring mold. Cover with aluminum foil and bake in the oven for 50 minutes. To test ring, pierce with a skewer – if it comes away cleanly the ring is cooked. Leave to cool before turning out.

To decorate, cut the fruits into even-sized pieces. Arrange them in center of ring. Whip cream and pipe 10 rosettes of cream around edge. Top with a sprig of mint.

Serves 8–10.

BLACK-CURRANT INDIVIDUALS

6 tablespoons black-currant preserve	
1 cup medium-fat curd cheese	
⅓ cup soured cream	
1 egg	
3 tablespoons sugar	
TO DECORATE:	
6 sprigs of mint	
TO SERVE:	
⅔ cup whipping cream	

Preheat oven to 350F. Spread 1 tablespoon black-currant preserve into bottom of 6 ramekin dishes. Place ramekins in a roasting pan and set aside.

In a bowl, beat cheese and soured cream. Add lemon peel and juice, egg and sugar, and beat until smooth. Spoon mixture into ramekin dishes, dividing it equally between them.

Pour enough boiling water into roasting pan to come halfway up sides of ramekin dishes. Bake in the oven for 35 minutes. Leave to cool completely.

To serve, run the blade of a small knife around edge of each ramekin dish and turn out on to a serving dish. Decorate each cheesecake with a sprig of mint and serve with loosely whipped cream.

Serves 6.

MANGO CHEESECAKE

¼ cup butter	
1⅓ cups graham craker crumbs	
FILLING:	
1 cup cream cheese	
⅔ cup plain yogurt	
⅔ cup soured cream	
2 eggs, separated	
⅓ cup superfine sugar	
1 tablespoon unflavored gelatin	
1⅓ cups raspberries	
TO DECORATE:	
14-ounce can mangos in syrup	
1⅓ cups raspberries	
⅔ cup whipping cream	
8–10 sprigs of mint	

Grease and line a 9-inch round, loose-bottomed cake tin. In a saucepan, melt butter, then stir in cracker crumbs. Mix well, then press into cake pan.

To make filling, beat cheese and yogurt in a bowl. Add sour cream, egg yolks and ¼ cup sugar and beat until smooth.

Sprinkle gelatin over 2 tablespoons water in a small bowl and leave to soften for 2–3 minutes. Stand the bowl in a saucepan of hot water and stir until dissolved and quite hot. Stir into cheese mixture.

Beat egg whites in a bowl with remaining sugar until firm. Fold into cheese mixture with the raspberries. Turn into cake pan and leave to set in the refrigerator for 2–3 hours.

To decorate, slice mango into thin strips and arrange in a fan shape on the top of the cheesecake. Arrange raspberries in center. Whip cream and pipe 8–10 rosettes around the edge. Top each with a sprig of mint.

Serves 8–10.

ICEBOX CHEESECAKE

⅓ cup butter

1⅔ cups plain cookie crumbs

½ teaspoon ground ginger

FILLING:

1 pound cream cheese

grated peel and juice of 1 lemon

4 eggs, separated

½ cup superfine sugar

4 teaspoons unflavored gelatin

1¼ cups whipping cream

TO DECORATE:

14-ounce can pineapple rings

1 heaped cup red cherries

angelica "leaves"

Grease and line an 8-inch round, loose-bottomed cake pan. In a saucepan, melt butter, then stir in crumbs. Mix well, then press into base of cake pan.

In a bowl, beat cheese, lemon peel and juice, egg yolks and ¼ cup superfine sugar until smooth.

Sprinkle gelatin over 2 table-spoons water in a small bowl and leave to soften for 2–3 minutes. Stand the bowl in a saucepan of hot water and stir until dissolved and quite hot. Stir into cheese mixture.

Loosely whip cream in a bowl and fold into cheese misture with a large metal spoon. In a separate bowl, beat egg whites with remaining sugar until firm, then fold into mixture. Pour on to crumb base and freeze in ice compartment for 4 hours.

To decorate, cut pineapple rings in half and arrange them around the edge of the cheesecake. Place a cherry and 2 angelica "leaves" in the center of every other ring.

Serves 8–10.

Note: This cheesecake can be served straight from the refrigerator.

RASPBERRY CHEESE ROLL

4 eggs

½ cup superfine sugar

½ cup blanched almonds, ground

2 tablespoons flour

FILLING:

¾ cup cream cheese

⅔ cup whipping cream

1 tablespoon confectioners' sugar

1 pound raspberries

TO DECORAE:

⅔ cup whipping cream

6–8 sprigs of mint

Preheat oven to 400F. Grease and line a 13- × 9-inch baking sheet. Beat eggs and sugar in a bowl until mixture is thick enough to hold trail of the mixer when beaters are lifted.

Sift ground almonds and flour over egg mixture and fold in with a large metal spoon. Spread out sponge mixture on the baking sheet and bake in the oven for 10–12 minutes or until springy to the touch. Turn out on to a wire rack and leave to cool.

Put cheese into a blender or food processor with cream and confec-tioners' sugar and blend until smooth – do not overblend or cream will separate.

Peel greaseproof paper off cake and spread cheese mixture over sponge. Scatter three-quarters of the raspberries over top, then roll up lightly.

To decorate, whip cream and pipe a row of rosettes along top of the cheese roll. Decorate with remaining raspberries and sprigs of mint.

Serves 6–8.

APRICOT CHEESECAKE

⅓ cup butter

1⅔ cups graham cracker crumbs

FILLING:

1 cup low-fat soft cheese

⅔ cup plain yogurt

¾ cup blanched almonds, ground

½ cup superfine sugar

⅔ cup whipping cream

1 tablespoon unflavored gelatin

2 eggs

few drops almond extract

TO DECORATE:

14-ounce can apricot halves

⅔ cup whipping cream

Grease and line an 8-inch square cake pan. In a saucepan, melt butter, then stir in cracker crumbs. Mix well, then press into base of cake pan.

In a bowl, beat cheese, yogurt, ground almonds and ¼ cup sugar until smooth. Loosely whip cream in a separate bowl, then fold into cheese mixture.

Sprinkle gelatin over 2 table-spoons water in a small bowl and leave to soften for 2–3 minutes. Stand the bowl in a saucepan of hot water and stir until dissolved and quite hot. Stir into cheese mixture. Beat eggs, almond extract and remaining sugar in a bowl until mixture is thick enough to hold trail of the mixer when beaters are lifted. Fold beaten eggs into cheese mixture and pour on to crumb base. Leave to set in the refrigerator for 2–3 hours.

To decorate, cut cheesecake into sixteen 2-inch squares. Drain apricot halves and place one in center of each square. Whip the cream around edge of each square.

Serves 6–8.

BLUEBERRY CHEESECAKE

½ cup butter

1½ cups graham cracker crumbs

2 tablespoons sweet sherry

FILLING:

2 cups ricotta cheese

⅔ cup plain yogurt

⅓ cup sugar

1 tablespoon lemon juice

2 eggs, separated

1 pound blueberries

1 tablespoon unflavored gelatin

TOPPING:

¼ cup red-currant jelly

TO SERVE:

sprigs of mint

⅔ cup whipping cream

Grease a 9-inch round, loose-bottomed cake pan. In a saucepan, melt butter, then stir in cracker crumbs and sherry. Mix well, then press into base of cake pan. Leave to firm in the refrigerator.

In a bowl, beat cheese, yogurt, ¼ cup sugar, lemon juice and egg yolks. Gently stir in ⅔ cup of the blueberries.

Sprinkle gelatin over 2 table-spoons water in a small bowl and leave to soften for 2–3 minutes. Stand the bowl in a saucepan of hot water and stir until dissolved and quite hot. Stir into cheese.

Beat egg whites with remaining sugar until firm and smooth. Fold into cheese mixture with a large metal spoon, then spoon on to crumb base. Leave to set in refrigerator for 2–3 hours.

To make topping, melt red-currant jelly in a small saucepan without boiling. Stir in remaining blueberries. Mix well, spread over cheesecake and chill. Decorate with mint and serve with whipped cream.

Serves 8–10.

COEURS À LA CRÈME

7 cups milk
2/3 cup whipping cream
1 1/2 teaspoons rennet
TO DECORATE:
2/3 whipping cream, if desired
1 1/3 cups strawberries

Line 6 coeur à la crème molds with a double layer of cheesecloth. Put milk and cream into a saucepan and warm to blood temperature (do not allow to become too hot or the milk will not curdle properly). Stir in rennet and leave for 1 hour.

When the milk has curdled, pour contents of saucepan into a preserving bag suspended over an upturned kitchen stool. Place a bowl underneath to collect the whey. Leave to drain for about 50 minutes.

Empty contents of preserving bag into a glass bowl and stir curds until smooth. Divide cheese between molds and leave in the refrigerator until firm.

Turn out on to individual serving plates. To decorate, if desired, whip cream, then pipe on to molds. Decorate with strawberry slices.

Serves 6.

REFRIGERATOR CHEESECAKE

1/3 cup butter
1 2/3 cups semi-sweet cookie crumbs
FILLING:
2 cups cream cheese
2/3 cup soured cream
2/3 cup plain yogurt
1/3 cup superfine sugar
3 eggs, separated
4 teaspoons unflavored gelatin
2/3 cup whipping cream
TOPPING:
1 pound assorted fresh fruits
2 tablespoons apple jelly, if desired

Grease and line an 8-inch round, loose-bottomed cake pan. In a saucepan, melt butter, then stir in cookie crumbs. Mix well, then press into base of cake pan.

In a bowl, beat cheese, soured cream, yogurt, 2 tablespoons superfine sugar and egg yolks until smooth.

Sprinkle gelatin over 2 tablespoons water in a small bowl and leave to soften for 2–3 minutes. Stand the bowl in a saucepan of hot water and stir until dissolved and quite hot. Stir into cheese.

Loosely whip cream in a bowl and fold into cheese. Beat egg whites with remaining sugar until firm, then fold into cheese. Turn into cake pan and leave to set in the refrigerator for 2–3 hours.

To decorate, cut fruits into even-sized pieces and arrange over top of cheesecake. Melt apple jelly and brush over the fruit to make a glaze, if desired.

Serves 8–10.

STRAWBERRY CHEESECAKES

¼ cup butter

1 ¼ cups graham cracker crumbs

FILLING:

1 ⅓ cups cream cheese

1 ¼ cups thick yogurt

2 egg yolks

⅓ cup superfine sugar

1 tablespoon unflavored gelatin

TOPPING:

1 pound strawberries

⅔ cup whipping cream

8 sprigs of mint

Place eight 3½-inch muffin rings on a cookie sheet and line with waxed paper. In a saucepan, melt butter, then stir in cracker crumbs. Mix well, press into bottom of each ring, dividing mixture equally.

In a bowl, beat cheese and yogurt. Add egg yolks and sugar and beat until smooth.

Sprinkle gelatin over 2 tablespoons water in a small bowl and leave to soften for 2–3 minutes. Stand the bowl in a saucepan of hot water and stir until dissolved and quite hot. Stir into cheese mixture. Pour into muffin rings and leave to set in the refrigerator for 2–3 hours before serving.

To decorate, slice strawberries and arrange over the cheesecakes. Whip cream and pipe a rosette of cream on to each cheesecake. Top each one with a sprig of mint.

Serves 8.

PEACH RASPBERRY CHEESECAKES

⅓ cup butter

1 ⅓ cups ginger cookie crumbs

FILLING:

½ cup cream cheese

½ cup thick yogurt

⅓ cup superfine sugar

⅔ cup whipping cream

4 teaspoons unflavored gelatin

14-ounce can sliced peaches, roughly chopped

2 eggs

TO DECORATE:

2 cups raspberries

⅔ cup whipping cream

2 tablespoons slivered almonds, flaked

Grease and line a 9-inch round, loose-bottomed cake pan. In a saucepan, melt butter, then stir in cookie crumbs. Mix well, then press into cake pan.

In a bowl, beat cheese, yogurt and 2 tablespoons sugar. Whip cream in a separate bowl and fold into cheese mixture.

Sprinkle gelatin over 2 tablespoons water in a small bowl and leave to soften for 2–3 minutes. Stand the bowl in a saucepan of hot water and stir into cheese mixture, then stir in chopped peaches.

Beat eggs and remaining sugar in a bowl until mixture is thick enough to hold trail of the mixer when beaters are lifted. Fold into cheese mixture. Turn into cake pan and leave to set in the refrigerator for 2–3 hours.

To decorate, arrange raspberries over surface, leaving a 1-inch border around the edge. In a bowl, whip cream and pipe rosettes on the uncovered border. Decorate each rosette with slivered almonds.

Serves 10.

ORANGE CHEESECAKE

⅓ cup butter	
4 ounces round baby's rusks, crushed	
¼ cup superfine sugar	
FILLING:	
1½ pound medium-fat soft cheese	
finely grated peel and juice of 1 orange	
2 eggs	
¼ cup superfine sugar	
TOPPING:	
14-ounce can mandarin orange segments	
2 tablespoons orange jelly	
mint leaves	

Preheat oven to 375F. Grease and line a 9-inch round, loose-bottomed cake pan. In a saucepan, melt butter, then stir in rusks and sugar. Mix well, then press into base and up sides of cake pan.

In a bowl, beat cheese, orange peel and juice, eggs and sugar until smooth. Turn into cake pan and bake in the oven for 40 minutes. Leave to cool before removing from pan.

To decorate, drain mandarin oranges on paper towels, then arrange on the top of cheesecake.

Make the ornage jelly and brush over mandarin oranges. Decorate each orange with a mint leaf.

Serves 8–10.

GOOSEBERRY CHEESECAKE

⅓ cup butter	
1¼ cups gratan cracker crumbs	
2 tablespoons sunflower seeds	
FILLING:	
1½ pounds medium-fat cheese	
juice of 1 lemon	
1 teaspoon orange flower water	
¼ cup superfine sugar	
TOPPING:	
14-ounce can gooseberries	
6 teaspoons cornstarch	
TO SERVE:	
cream or yogurt	

Preheat oven to 375F. Grease and line a 9-inch round, loose-bottomed cake pan. In a saucepan, melt butter, then stir in cracker crumbs and sunflower seeds. Mix well, then press into cake pan.

In a bowl, beat cheese, lemon juice, orange flower water, eggs and sugar. Turn into cake pan and bake in the oven for 40 minutes. Leave to cool.

Meanwhile, make topping. Drain gooseberries and put juice into a small saucepan. Bring to a boil. Mix cornstarch with 4 tablespoons water. Stir into gooseberry juice and simmer to thicken. Add gooseberries, stir gently, then spread over cheesecake.

When cheesecake is cold, remove from pan and serve with cream or yogurt.

Serves 8–10.

RED-CURRANT CHEESECAKE

LIQUEUR CHEESECAKE

¼ cup butter

1¼ cups graham cracker crumbs

FILLING:

1½ pound medium-fat cheese

finely grated peel and juice of 1 orange

2 eggs

¼ cup superfine sugar

2 cups red-currants, thawed if frozen

TOPPING:

¼ cup red-currant jelly

8-10 sprigs of mint

Preheat oven to 375F. Grease and line a 9-inch round, loose-bottomed cake pan. In a saucepan, melt butter, then stir in cracker crumbs.

Mix well, then press into cake pan.

In a bowl, beat cheese, lemon peel and juice, eggs and sugar. Stir ⅔ cup of the red-currants into cheese mixture. Turn into cake pan and bake in the oven for 45 minutes.

To make topping, melt red-currant jelly in a saucepan. Stir in remaining red-currants and spread over surface of cheesecake. Leave the cheesecake to cool before removing from pan. Decorate with sprigs of mint.

Serves 8–10.

⅓ cup butter

1⅔ cups graham cracker crumbs

FILLING:

1 pound ricotta cheese

1⅔ cup soured cream

3 eggs

1 tablespoon flour

⅓ cup soft brown sugar

finely grated peel and juice of 2 oranges

⅓ cup Grand Marnier

TO DECORATE

3 small oranges

⅔ cup whipping cream

1⅓ cups strawberries

Preheat oven to 375F. Grease and line a 9-inch round, spring-form cake pan. In a saucepan, melt butter, then stir in cracker crumbs. Mix well, then press into cake pan.

In a bowl, beat cheese, soured cream, eggs, flour and sugar. Add orange peel and juice and Grand Marnier and beat until smooth. Turn into cake pan and bake in the oven for 50 minutes. Leave to cool before removing the cheesecake from the pan.

To decorate, cut oranges into ¼ inch slices. Make a cut from center to edge of each slice, then hold slice at each side of cut and twist to form as S shape. Arrange orange twists around edge of cheesecake.

Whip cream in a bowl, then pipe a rosette of cream into each orange twist and add a strawberry.

Serves 8–10.

CAMPARI CHEESECAKE

1/3 cup butter
1 2/3 cups plain cookie crumbs
FILLING:
1 cup low-fat soft cheese
2/3 cup plain yogurt
2/3 cup whipping cream
finely grated peel and juice of 1 pink grapefruit
1/3 cup Campari
4 teaspoons unflavored gelatin
2 eggs
TO DECORATE
2 kiwi fruit
2 pink grapefruit, peeled and divided into segments
5 maraschino cherries, halved

Grease and line a 8-inch round, loose-bottomed cake pan. In a saucepan, melt butter, then stir in cookie crumbs. Mix well, then press into base of cake pan.

In a bowl, cream until smooth. Add grapefruit peel and juice and Campari and beat until smooth.

Sprinkle gelatin over 2 tablespoons water in a small bowl and leave to soften for 2–3 minutes. Stand bowl in a saucepan of hot water and stir until dissolved. Stir into cheese mixture.

Beat eggs and sugar in a bowl until mixture is thick enough to hold trail of the mixer when beaters are lifted. Fold beaten eggs into cheese mixture, then turn into cake pan. Leave to set in the refrigerator for 2–3 hours.

To decorate, slice kiwi fruit. Turn out cheesecake and arrange segments of grapefruit, slices of kiwi fruit and maraschino cherries around the edge.

Serves 8–10.

TIPSY CHEESECAKE

1/3 cup butter
1 2/3 cups plain cookie crumbs
FILLING:
2 ounces macaroons
1/3 cup dry sherry
1 1/2 cups medium-fat cheese
2/3 cup whipping cream
2 eggs
1/3 cup superfine sugar
1 pound raspberries
2 tablespoons confectioners' sugar

Put the macaroons for the filling into a small bowl. Pour over the sherry and leave to soak for 15–20 minutes until sherry is absorbed.

Meanwhile, preheat oven to 350F. Grease and line an 8-inch round, loose-bottomed cake pan. In a saucepan, melt butter, then stir in cookie crumbs. Mix well, then press into base of cake pan.

In a bowl, beat cheese, cream, eggs and superfine sugar until smooth (do not overbeat or cheesecake will rise during baking).

Stir macaroons into mixture, trying not to break them up. Stir in 1 cup of the raspberries. Turn into cake pan and bake in the oven for 50 minutes. Leave to cool before removing from pan.

To decorate, dust surface of cheesecake with confectioners' sugar and arrange remaining raspberries around edge in 3 rows.

Serves 6–8.

WHITE CHOCOLATE CAKE

¼ cup butter

1¼ cups chocolate graham cracker crumbs

FILLING:

1½ cups ricotta cheese

1 cup sweet chestnut purée

⅔ cup whipping cream

white chocolate, broken into pieces

2 tablespoons brandy

3 eggs

1 tablespoon flour

TO DECORATE

4 ounces white chocolate

⅔ cup whipping cream

10 pieces candied chestnut

superfine sugar

10 angelica "leaves"

Preheat oven to 350F. Grease and line an 8-inch round, loose-bottomed cake pan. In a saucepan, melt butter, then stir in cracker crumbs. Mix well and press into base of cake pan.

In a bowl, beat cheese and chestnut purée. Bring cream to a boil in a small saucepan. Remove from heat, add chocolate and stir until melted. Add brandy and stir into cheese mixture. Add eggs and flour and beat well. Turn into cake pan and bake in the oven for 1 hour. Leave to cool before removing from pan.

To decorate, grate white chocolate over surface of cheesecake. Whip cream and pipe a border of 10 large rosettes around edge and decorate with pieces of candied chestnut rolled in superfine sugar and each topped with angelica "leaves".

Serves 8–10.

CHOC & WHISKEY CHEESECAKE

¼ cup butter

1⅔ cups ginger cookie crumbs

FILLING:

1½ pounds cream cheese

¼ cup soft brown sugar

2 eggs

2 tablespoons cocoa powder

2 teaspoons ground ginger

⅔ cup whipping cream

8 ounces bitter chocolate, broken into pieces

⅓ cup whiskey

TO DECORATE

6 teaspoons cocoa powder

4 teaspoons confectioners' sugar

½ teaspoon ground ginger

Preheat oven to 350F. Grease and line an 8-inch round, loose-bottomed cake pan. In a saucepan, melt butter, then stir in cookie crumbs. Mix well, then press into base of cake pan.

To make filling, beat together cheese, brown sugar and eggs in a bowl. Sift in cocoa powder and ginger and beat until smooth. Bring cream to a boil in a small saucepan. Remove from heat, add chocolate and stir until melted. Stir in whiskey and blend into cheese mixture.

Turn into cake pan and bake in the oven for 45 minutes. Leave to cool before removing from cake pan.

To decorate, cut out 5 strips of greaseproof paper ¾-inch wide and lay them at intervals over surface of cheesecake. Mix together cocoa powder, confectioners' sugar and ground ginger, then sift over cake. Carefully remove strips and serve at once.

Serves 8–10.

RICH CHOCOLATE CHEESECAKES

⅓ cup butter

1⅓ cups chocolate-coated graham cracker crumbs

FILLING:

1½ pounds cream cheese

3 eggs

¼ cup dark soft brown sugar

3 tablespoons molasses or black treacle

2 tablespoons cocoa powder

1 teaspoon ground allspice

finely grated peel and juice of 1 orange

⅔ cup whipping cream

8 ounces bitter chocolate, broken into pieces

¼ cup soft unsalted butter

TOPPING:

8 ounces bitter chocolate, flaked

4 ounces white chocolate, flaked

Preheat oven to 350F. Grease and line a 9-inch round, loose-bottomed cake pan. In a saucepan, melt butter, then stir in crumbs. Mix, then press into pan.

In a bowl, beat cheese, eggs, sugar, molasses or black treacle, cocoa powder, allspice, orange peel and juice. Bring cream to a boil in a small saucepan. Remove from the heat, add chocolate and stir until melted. Beat in butter, then blend into cheese mixture.

Turn into cake pan and bake in the oven for 50 minutes. Leave to cool before removing from pan.

To decorate, arrange bitter chocolate flakes in overlapping layers around edge of cake, alternating with the 2 colored chocolates toward the center.

Serves 10.

LEMON MERINGUE POSSET

½ cup butter

2¼ cups graham cracker crumbs

FILLING:

3 egg yolks

1¾ cups heavy cream

juice of 2 lemons

⅓ cup superfine sugar

TOPPING:

3 egg whites

2 tablespoons superfine sugar, plus extra for sprinkling

lemon twist and sprig of mint

Grease and line an 8-inch tart pan. In a saucepan, melt butter, then stir in cracker crumbs. Mix well, then press into base and up sides of tart pan.

In a bowl, beat egg yolks until pale in color. Bring cream to a boil in a saucepan. Add lemon juice and sugar. Beat into egg yolks, then spoon on to cracker base. Leave to set in the refrigerator for 2–3 hours.

To make topping, beat egg whites in a bowl with the sugar until stiff, then pile on to the tart. Sprinkle with sugar and brown under a hot broiler. Decorate with mint and lemon twist.

Serves 8–10.

INDEX